Identity and the Young
English Language Learner

BILINGUAL EDUCATION AND BILINGUALISM
Series Editors: Professor Colin Baker, *University of Wales, Bangor, Wales, Great Britain*
and Professor Nancy H. Hornberger, *University of Pennsylvania, Philadelphia, USA*

Other Books in the Series
At War With Diversity: US Language Policy in an Age of Anxiety
  James Crawford
Bilingual Education and Social Change
  Rebecca Freeman
Cross-linguistic Influence in Third Language Acquisition
  J. Cenoz, B. Hufeisen and U. Jessner (eds)
Dual Language Education
  Kathryn J. Lindholm-Leary
English in Europe: The Acquisition of a Third Language
  Jasone Cenoz and Ulrike Jessner (eds)
Foundations of Bilingual Education and Bilingualism
  Colin Baker
An Introductory Reader to the Writings of Jim Cummins
  Colin Baker and Nancy Hornberger (eds)
Japanese Children Abroad: Cultural, Educational and Language Issues
  Asako Yamada-Yamamoto and Brian Richards (eds)
Language Minority Students in the Mainstream Classroom (2nd Edition)
  Angela L. Carrasquillo and Vivian Rodriguez
Learning English at School: Identity, Social Relations and Classroom Practice
  Kelleen Toohey
Language, Power and Pedagogy: Bilingual Children in the Crossfire
  Jim Cummins
Language Revitalization Processes and Prospects
  Kendall A. King
Language Use in Interlingual Families: A Japanese-English Sociolinguistic Study
  Masayo Yamamoto
Learners' Experiences of Immersion Education: Case Studies of French and Chinese
  Michèle de Courcy
Power, Prestige and Bilingualism: International Perspectives on Elite Bilingual
Education
  Anne-Marie de Mejía
Reflections on Multiliterate Lives
  Diane Belcher and Ulla Connor (eds)
The Sociopolitics of English Language Teaching
  Joan Kelly Hall and William G. Eggington (eds)
World English: A Study of its Development
  Janina Brutt-Griffler

Please contact us for the latest book information:
Multilingual Matters, Frankfurt Lodge, Clevedon Hall,
Victoria Road, Clevedon, BS21 7HH, England
http://www.multilingual-matters.com

BILINGUAL EDUCATION AND BILINGUALISM 36
Series Editors: Colin Baker and Nancy H. Hornberger

Identity and the Young English Language Learner

Elaine Mellen Day

MULTILINGUAL MATTERS LTD
Clevedon • Buffalo • Toronto • Sydney

To my mother

Library of Congress Cataloging in Publication Data
A catalog record for this book is available from the Library of Congress.

British Library Cataloguing in Publication Data
A catalogue entry for this book is available from the British Library.

ISBN 1-85359-598-5 (hbk)
ISBN 1-85359-597-7 (pbk)

Multilingual Matters Ltd
UK: Frankfurt Lodge, Clevedon Hall, Victoria Road, Clevedon BS21 7HH.
USA: UTP, 2250 Military Road, Tonawanda, NY 14150, USA.
Canada: UTP, 5201 Dufferin Street, North York, Ontario M3H 5T8, Canada.
Australia: Footprint Books, PO Box 418, Church Point, NSW 2103, Australia.

Printed and bound in Great Britain by the Cromwell Press Ltd.

Contents

Acknowledgments

I would like to thank all those who assisted me in the preparation of this work. I would like to express deep appreciation to Kelleen Toohey, Project Director, who gave unsparingly of her time and support and guided me during all phases of the project. I would also like to thank Diane Dagenais and Stan Shapson for their generous support and assistance in my work. I benefited from my association with Sarah Yip, a member of the research team with whom I worked during the data collection period. Linda Hof deserves special mention for her excellent work in videotaping the classroom. I am very grateful to bilingual researchers Kunwal Aurora and Bozena Karwowska for their roles in conducting the home study. I would also like to warmly thank Roumiana Ilieva, Barbara Muthwa-Kuehn, and Bonnie Waterstone for research assistance, Lisa Day for transcribing the video transcripts, and Lynn Reader for technical assistance. My appreciation is extended to Bonny Norton for many illuminating discussions in her seminar on language and identity. I am very grateful to Aneta Pavlenko for her invaluable recommendations for improving the manuscript. I am also very grateful to John Holt for his excellent professional advice and careful editing of the manuscript. I profited from the financial support provided to this project by the Social Sciences and Humanities Research Council of Canada.

Above all, I would like to thank the teacher, children, and families who participated in this project; without their full and generous cooperation, this study would not have been feasible. And last but not least, I would like to thank my family for their love and encouragement. My husband, Rod, deserves special recognition for his critical eye and his patience, love and support during all the phases of my work.

Chapter 1
Introduction

In recent years, there has been increasing discussion of the need for the researcher to be reflexive, to declare her investment and interest in the research. The researcher's personal biography cannot remain disassociated from the research; the period in which that research takes place, the researcher's social location and her access to theories play key roles in motivating and framing the research (Skeggs, 1995). Hence, I begin this work with a brief personal introduction.

I am the child of Greek parents who immigrated from Greece to the United States before World War II and settled in the city of Boston in the north-eastern United States. Greek was the language we spoke at home. I do not know whether I would have been classified as an 'ESL child' in the sense of knowing little English upon entering kindergarten. I do not think so, as I had older siblings who spoke English; however, I certainly would have been classified as a 'minority language child'; that is, a child coming from a home in which the family used a language other than English.

My learning our home language, Greek, was very important to my family. Hence, during the elementary school years I attended Greek school twice a week after school. Religion also played an important part in our lives, and I attended church and Sunday school weekly at the Greek Orthodox Church. This situation meant that I had at least three peer social networks, two of which (Greek and Sunday school) overlapped, and one of which (the public school) did not.

I remember as far back as my kindergarten days sensing that there were differences between my family and those of my classmates, most of whom were Irish Catholic. Although we sometimes played in one another's homes, where whatever differences existed might have become obvious, I can remember being careful to hide some aspects of my Greek identity from my 'American school' friends. I would not, for example, tell them that I spoke Greek or went to Greek school, and I managed to escape (a verb that describes my feelings at the time) doing so until I was about ten years old.

At that age, four or five of my 'American school' friends and I had decided to form a club which would meet weekly in our homes. One of the two meeting days proposed was a Greek school day; I remember

1

struggling over whether I should tell my friends the real reason I could not meet on that day or whether I should make up some excuse. I decided on the former and came later to look on this act of identity as a critical turning point in my life.

Like most North American school children, I did not receive in elementary school any encouragement or praise for learning my home language. Gutierrez and Larson's (1994) description of Latino children in California leaving their 'maletas' behind when they entered school accords with my own experience. However, in my secondary school, an academically oriented girls' school drawing from the entire urban population and therefore quite diverse in terms of the students' sociocultural backgrounds, some of my teachers positively reinforced those of us who came from immigrant backgrounds and could speak other languages. I remember liking this at the time and I think that this positive recognition made a difference to my perceptions of who I was.

Not until I carried out the observations for the present study of English language learners had I ever personally questioned or confronted the fact that my home language and bilingual skills were *not* recognized in my elementary school years. One day at around the time of Chinese New Year, one little girl from a Chinese home background had drawn two Chinese characters, which the teacher posted on the bulletin board. I wrote in my field notes and explored in my journal:

> Sarah so pleased about her Chinese characters. My moment of consciousness! I was so pleased with the recognition we got in high school about speaking our home languages. But now I see: No one ever recognized in elementary school that I could write Greek! (February 1997).

Bourdieu (1991) uses the term 'symbolic domination' to refer to 'the ability of certain social groups to maintain control over others by establishing their view of reality and their cultural practices as the most valued, and, perhaps more importantly, as the norm' (Heller, 1995: 373). The neglect and denial of children's home languages was and continues to be a very emotional issue for me. Perhaps because I was afraid that my emotions would intrude too much, I did not take up the issue of home language recognition fully in this work, though I have done so elsewhere (Dagenais & Day, 1998, 1999).

I have always loved languages and studied them avidly, both at school and through self-study and travel. As an undergraduate at Harvard-Radcliffe, I majored in Ancient Greek and Latin and then taught Latin and English in secondary school in Massachusetts. When I later moved to British Columbia, I did a Master's degree in French linguistics at

Simon Fraser University and also taught French there. Out of personal background and interest, I have always believed in the benefits of learning languages and have had an enduring interest in and commitment to second language education, in my personal life, as an advocate in my own community, and in my professional life, a large part of which has been devoted to research into French immersion education.

Starting in the late 1970s and continuing until the early 1990s, I worked in a research unit devoted to French language education, based at Simon Fraser University. There, I collaborated with my colleague, Stan Shapson, and others on a wide variety of studies on French immersion, covering the areas of evaluation and assessment, curriculum and instruction, and teacher education. Much of our work was for school districts and government agencies in the days when the Canadian French immersion program was experimental and when bilingualism carried negative associations in the eyes of the general public. My experience in this context was with research as practice, in that the questions we asked were to a certain extent determined by and accountable to a whole network of groups and individuals, both in the public at large and in the educational system, who were concerned with determining the French immersion program's effectiveness, its suitability for different students, and areas where it needed change and improvement.

We used a range of research methodologies and approaches, including experimental, survey, case study, and other qualitative approaches (see Day & Shapson, 1996). As Cumming (1994) points out:

> decisions to utilize any one research orientation ... pose a unique, contextually based set of decisions requiring careful consideration of the orientation to research itself, the situation and resources at hand, and the purposes to be achieved (p. 697).

Through work in French immersion teacher education, in particular, I became more familiar with the philosophic orientation underlying research under the broad rubric of 'naturalism' (Hammersley & Atkinson, 1983), and my work became increasingly oriented that way. In addition, more recent qualitative studies in which we observed classrooms also forced me to face issues in doing qualitative research, including grappling with issues of power relations and of taking a visualist stance on other people and representing them through text. These I consider very problematic; although I had hoped that I could somehow overcome them, I cannot claim to have done so in this work.

Contemporary researchers discuss many sources of influence on their research, such as their personal experiences, cultural ideologies and philosophical and ethical commitments. The intellectual biography of the researcher influences the research and has to be openly acknowledged (Goetz & LeCompte, 1984). Before undertaking this study, I had read some ethnographic work on bilingual programs in the United States (e.g., Saravia-Shore & Arvizu, 1992) in connection with a study of French immersion children with home languages other than English or French, on which I was collaborating with Diane Dagenais (Dagenais & Day, 1998, 1999). These readings dovetailed nicely with some of the readings I was doing on sociocultural and poststructural theories in connection with my doctoral studies in second language education.

Thus, when Kelleen Toohey, my senior supervisor, received funding in 1996 to continue her ethnographic project on English language learners and asked me if I was interested in joining, I gladly accepted because I wanted to work with the sociocultural research perspectives I was reading about and in an area (English language learning) different from the one in which I had worked before.[1] I also joined for pragmatic reasons (this project already had secure funding and an administrative structure established) and for social ones (Kelly was a person I felt I could trust and with whom I could have a collegial research relationship such as the one I had been used to). A more fundamental consideration related to values. One day, Kelly told me about some of her experiences in her research project and her conviction of its importance, saying of the English language learners she had been studying: 'No one speaks for them.' Her emotional tone of conviction and commitment convinced me that hers was a project on which I would want to work. This conviction, and our shared interests in broader philosophical issues related to the individualizing of children in schools and in alternative perspectives proposed by philosophers (Taylor, 1989), researchers (Lave, 1996; McDermott, 1993) and educators (Paley, 1992), inspired the research that led to this book.

The Project

The ethnographic project from which this research draws follows two cohorts of English language learners enrolled in mainstream Canadian primary classrooms from kindergarten through Grade 2. Kelly Toohey, the director, initiated the project in 1994, with the purposes of documenting the school experiences over time of several children learning English as a second language, specifically investigating classroom activities and practices and how these create possibilities for engagement in particular kinds of conversations (Toohey, 2000).

The project was conducted in an elementary school in a rapidly growing suburb close to Vancouver, British Columbia, Canada's most western province. It included weekly observations of two cohorts of children in their classrooms, monthly videotaping, document collection, teacher interviews, and interviews with the families and children in their homes. The first cohort of six children (three boys, three girls) was observed from the beginning of kindergarten to the end of Grade 2 (1994 to 1997). The second cohort of five children (one boy, four girls) was observed in kindergarten and in Grade 1 (1996 to 1998). The children's home language backgrounds are Chinese, Polish, and Punjabi.

I joined the project in September 1996, when the first cohort (Cohort 1) was beginning Grade 2 and the second cohort (Cohort 2) kindergarten. Another researcher, Sarah Yip, also joined the project at that time. Sarah and I worked with Kelly as a research team, conducting observations in both cohorts, but I assumed major responsibility for the observations of the Cohort 2 children in kindergarten and continued my observations of them through Grade 1.

Kelly's study (Toohey, 2000) of Cohort 1 followed the six children from kindergarten through Grade 2, focusing on: (a) identity practices in kindergarten; (b) physical, material and intellectual resource distribution practices in Grade 1; and (c) instructional practices in Grade 2. My study, which draws from data on the Cohort 2 children while in kindergarten, follows the learning trajectory of one child, a Punjabi-speaking boy to whom I give the pseudonym Hari, over the course of one year in the context of his relations with others in his classroom. My study centrally concerns identity practices and their effects on access to language. My personal background as a 'minority language child' undoubtedly drove me to probe into the lived experience of one child alone as it concerned these topics.

Approaches

Although Kelly (Toohey, 2000) and I both deal with similar issues, we have somewhat different foci. With respect to the question of access, Kelly concentrates on teacher practices that regulate children's access to material, linguistic, social and other mediating resources, whereas I concentrate on the dynamics of classroom relationships. With respect to identity practices, she uses a social construction analysis to show how specific kinds of students (e.g., 'ESL') are constructed through labeling, evaluation, and ranking practices. I bring together sociocultural and poststructural approaches to probe into the relation between individual and social processes, exploring a current dilemma in the conceptualization of the social human person aptly expressed by Lemke (1995) as:

how to have an active, creative human subject which constructs social meanings, at the same time that this subject itself must be a social construction (quoted in John-Steiner & Mahn, 1996: 196).

Preview

In Chapter 2, I describe the theoretical framework for the study, which includes Bakhtin's (1981, 1984a,b, 1986) and Vygotsky's (1978, 1986) theories on language and learning, the work of contemporary sociocultural theorists on situated learning (Lave & Wenger, 1991), and poststructural theories on identity (Henriques *et al.*, 1984; Weedon, 1987); I also summarize recent ethnographic literature related to my work. In Chapter 3, I provide a brief account of how I conducted the study. In Chapter 4, I present background and contextual information on Hari's school, teacher, and classroom and on Hari himself, describing how he made use of his home language and his English and the changes I observed over the year. In the subsequent chapters, I explore the intimate connection between learning, identity, and social membership by examining Hari's relationships with his peers and teacher, using themes derived from my theoretical framework. These themes include social relations, participation, positioning, appropriation, and identification.

In Chapter 5, I first examine Hari's relationship with Kevin, one of the children with whom Hari affiliated in the beginning months of the school year. In the second section, I examine how Hari participates with the larger sub-group of children of which the two boys were a part. I also examine the identities he displays in different social networks and in different oral practices. In the last section, I analyze power relations and positioning practices to show the kinds of identities on offer to Hari and to help understand the kinds of participation I observed. I also examine strategies Hari uses in responding to the positions assigned to him and how he negotiates a more powerful identity.

In Chapter 6, I trace the development of Hari's relationship with Casey, a boy who was a newcomer to the class in late January. As in Chapter 5, I analyze social and political aspects of their relationship, but I focus more closely on questions of identity and language appropriation, showing the kinds of positions on offer to Hari, the identities available to him and how these affected his possibilities for appropriating language.

In Chapter 7, I examine Hari's relationship and interactions with his teacher, Mrs Clark. In the first section, I focus on Hari's participation in circle activities. In the second section, I examine the teacher's discourse, revealing her construction of Hari and his positioning as student. In the final section, I suggest that Hari plays his own role in maintaining and enhancing the position offered to him by the teacher. The final chapter (Chapter 8) contains a summary discussion, conclusions, and practical and theoretical implications. Overall, I stress the importance of social relationships in learning, highlighting both power and affective dynamics in these relationships and their unconscious as well as conscious dimensions.

Notes

1. Following Toohey (2000), I have adopted the term English language learner to refer to children learning English as a second language, because of the controversy attached to the label ESL.

Chapter 2
Theory and Literature

> I have tried elsewhere to draw attention to the hegemony of the view
> that learning is a matter of an increase in or reorganization of knowl-
> edge.... This dominant concern with epistemological issues precludes
> any reference to changes in practice or changes in *being* ...
>
> (Packer, 1993: 264)

Indirectly, the Cartesian assumption of the separateness of mind and body
and of self and other underlies most twentieth-century linguistics and
mainstream second language acquisition (SLA) research (Marková &
Foppa, 1990). More particularly, the assumptions underlying SLA research
derive from a conceptualization of language developed by the Swiss
philologist and linguist Ferdinand de Saussure, whose work forms the
basis for much of twentieth-century linguistic thought. Saussure aimed to
establish language study as a science; to do so, he posited 'an object of study
given in advance of scientific investigation, in other words, a reality
existing independently of its study and free from human beliefs, intentions,
and feelings' (Dunn & Lantolf, 1998: 425). This object of study, *'langue,'*
constituted a rule-governed closed system of signs to be studied separately
from *'parole,'* or language as social practice, which Saussure considered
unsystematic and not amenable to scientific investigation. Saussure also
gave precedence to the contemporary rather than historical study of
language ('synchrony' as opposed to 'diachrony').

More recently, Chomsky (1957, 1965) drew a distinction between
competence, the knowledge of a language possessed by an idealized native
speaker-hearer, and performance, the actual use of language in concrete
situations. This distinction between knowing and using language has
formed the basis for much work in mainstream SLA research.[1]

As a consequence of these underpinnings, much SLA research rests on
an information-processing model of language and communication and the
'conduit metaphor' (Reddy, 1979). This assumes that 'minds are containers
and that language itself is also a container, into which speakers insert
meanings that they transmit to listeners, who subsequently unpackage the
containers, extract the meanings and insert them into their own minds'

(Dunn & Lantolf, 1998: 424). The input–output computational metaphor is related to this (Lantolf, 1996).

However, several recent researchers (e.g., Bourne, 1988; Norton Peirce, 1989, 1993; Norton, 2000; Norton & Toohey, 2001; Pennycook, 1990, 2001) have criticized work in SLA and applied linguistics generally on the grounds that it promotes an idealist view of language divorced from its social, political, and historical context. They argue that the dichotomies created by twentieth century linguistics between *'langue'* and *'parole,'* competence and performance, and synchrony and diachrony, have promoted a view of language as an abstract system removed from social, cultural, political, and historical factors and of language acquisition as a biological, individual process rather than a social one.

Mainstream SLA Research

In mainstream SLA research, learning is seen as an individual process that takes place in the learner's mind. Much research has concentrated on tracing the learner's linguistic route of development and positing internal psychological mechanisms to account for this (e.g., Dulay *et al.*, 1982). These mechanisms, thought to be universal among learners, are conceptualized as an innate, language-specific faculty in one strand of research, called 'universal grammar' (e.g., White, 1989), or as more general learning mechanisms in other 'cognitive' strands (e.g., Corder, 1967; Selinker, 1972).

Other research streams have focused on the language learner and investigated how learner differences might affect language learning (e.g., Gardner, 1985; Wong Fillmore, 1979). Such research conceptualizes these differences as fixed characteristics or traits such as aptitude, motivation, or learning style, and sees them as potentially influencing the rate or ultimate outcome of learning, but not the developmental path, which supposedly remains universal for all learners. Some researchers have also investigated social and cultural factors (e.g., Schumann, 1978a, 1978b), but have considered these as external to the learner and playing a marginal role in language learning.

In the 1980s, a major line of research, called 'interactionist,' developed around the question of how learners' linguistic experience might contribute to language learning. Initially, Krashen (1981) claimed that comprehensible input is the critical variable in language learning (comprehensible input hypothesis); later Swain (1985) claimed that language learners also need to produce language to learn (output hypothesis). These arguments stimulated researchers to examine learners' interactions with their interlocutors and to show how negotiation of meaning in these interactions played a central role both in making input comprehensible and in providing occasions for productive output (e.g., Ellis, 1990; Gass & Madden, 1985; Pica, 1994; Swain, 1985).

In recent years, researchers working from a variety of more socially oriented traditions, including critical discourse analysis and critical sociolinguistics (e.g., Firth & Wagner, 1997 and Rampton, 1991, 1995); feminist poststuctural theory (e.g., Norton, 2000; Norton & Toohey, 2001), and sociocultural theory (e.g., Dunn & Lantolf, 1998; Hall, 1995, 1997; Hall & Verplaetse, 2000; Lantolf, 2000; Lantolf & Appel, 1994a; Platt & Brooks, 1994; van Lier, 2000), have challenged the cognitive, individualist assumptions shared by these research approaches and their dominance in the field of second language learning. They argue that SLA needs to be reconceptualized to include a far broader range of perspectives, in particular those which privilege context, discourse and interaction, complexify the view of the language learner, and seek interpretive understandings of the complexity and particularity of learning.

Critics also argue that the emphasis in educational research on the cognitive, individual aspects of learning has meant that until recently, little serious consideration has been given to the social nature of self or the sociality of learning (e.g., Davis, 1995; Toohey, 1998, 2000; Willett, 1995). These concerns stem from an intellectual stream that has its source in the work of the Soviet psychologist Lev S. Vygotsky (1896–1934) and the literary critic and semiotician Mikhail M. Bakhtin (1895–1975).

Language as Dialogic

Bakhtin opposes Saussure's view of language as a closed system and his dichotomous distinctions between language and speech, individual and society, and self and other. Bakhtin argues that discourse and meaning are fundamentally social; he writes of language development as a process whereby learners appropriate and transform the language of specific people with whom they interact:

> Words are, initially, the other's words, and at foremost, the mother's words. Gradually, these 'alien words' change, dialogically, to become one's 'own alien words' until they are transformed into 'one's own words.' (Bakhtin, 1984a, cited in Smolka *et al.*, 1995: 181)

Bakhtin stresses the situatedness of language in particular social, historical, cultural, and economic environments. In contrast to Saussure, for whom linguistic form and meaning abstracted from actual conditions of use constitute the object of study, Bakhtin (1986) argues that the *utterance*, not the word or sentence, should be the object of analysis: 'For speech can exist in reality only in the form of concrete utterances of individual speaking people, speech subjects' (p. 71). For Bakhtin, utterances can exist only through a *voice*, which refers to the socially situated speaking person and encompasses such factors as a speaking person's perspective, world view, values, and relationship to the voices of others.

In Bakhin's view, an utterance can be studied meaningfully only as an inseparable element of verbal communication; for him, the principle of dialogicality is fundamental. Dialogicality stresses both the mutual role of addressee and speaker in the construction of utterances and the connectedness of human speech communication, not only in present inter-actions but also in past and future discourses.

Bakhtin stresses that an utterance is dialogic as an actual dialogue between interlocutors, as inner dialogue among the voices in our heads, and as a dialogue 'with that anonymous and disembodied social Other' in our languages and the social horizons they project (Morgan, 1987: 455). He writes of 'an intense interaction and struggle between one's own and another's word' that takes place in the utterance, 'a process in which they oppose or dialogically interanimate each other' (Bakhtin, 1981: 354).

For Bakhtin, when we use language, we not only respond to a particular interaction or move it along but we also indicate our stance and negotiate our place and positioning toward the others involved (Hall, 1995). In this view, as Hall summarizes:

> 'Acquiring a language' or 'becoming competent' is not a matter of learning to speak. It is, instead, a matter of developing a range of voices, of learning to *ventriloquate* i.e., to (re) construct utterances for our own purposes from the resources available to us (Bakhtin 1986: 96), within and through our social identities, in the many and varied inter-active practices through which we live our lives. (1995: 218)

In our communicative activity with others, we have the opportunity for symbolic freedom as we struggle to create our own voice from the resources given and in response to the voices of others. By using language creatively, we can exercise our individual voice and challenge the world we encounter (Hall, 1993a, 1993b, 1995).

Bakhtin is concerned with linguistic variation (which he terms heteroglossia), conflict, and human intentionality, and he stresses the complexities of finding a voice in heteroglossic speech situations where voices (and the roles they express in the social structure) struggle for influ-ence within an individual's consciousness (Cazden, 1989, 1992). He wishes to transcend the dualism between language and speech and between individual and society, and he emphasizes the dialectal relations between them. Bakhtin's emphasis on the interdependence of the individual and social and the importance of social history for understanding learning was paralleled in psychology by the work of Vygotsky (1978, 1986).

Learning as Social

Vygotsky sees development not as the unfolding of innate capacities (a view prevalent in mainstream SLA research) but as the transformation of these capacities once they intertwine with socioculturally constructed mediational means (Lantolf & Pavlenko, 1995). Wertsch (1991) identifies three major themes throughout Vygotsky's work: (a) a reliance on a genetic or developmental method for understanding learning; (b) the claim that individual development, including higher mental functioning, has its origins in social activity; and (c) the claim that human mental action is mediated by tools (technical tools) and signs (psychological tools).

In Vygotsky's view, we must try to understand the nature of mental processes not by analyzing the products of development but by examining their origin and the transitions they have undergone. According to him, it is crucial to study the historical processes of development in all its phases and changes, for, 'It is only in movement that a body shows what it is' (Vygotsky, 1978: 65). In elaborating his methodological approach, Vygotsky emphasizes that the process of learning must be studied not as a general phenomenon but in the specific cultural and social contexts in which it occurs. He also emphasizes that development should be seen as highly complex and dynamic, arising from a complex dialectical process which is uneven, abrupt, erratic and marked by qualitative revolutionary changes.

Vygotsky (1978) also sees play as leading development. He gives imagination a central role, writing: 'The old adage that child's play is imagination in action must be reversed: we can say that imagination in adolescents and school children is play without action' (p. 93).

The social dimension of learning is primordial for Vygotsky, as is evident in his well-known genetic law of cultural development:

> Every function in the child's cultural development appears twice: first, on the social level, and later, on the individual level; first, *between* people (*interpsychological*), and then *inside* the child (*intrapsychological*).... All the higher functions originate as actual relations between human individuals. (Vygotsky, 1978: 57; italics in original)

For Vygotsky, cognitive processes occur first on the social plane; these shared processes are then internalized, transformed to the individual plane. Language learning thus comprises the internalization of the language of social interaction from inter-psychological to intra-psychological processes.

Vygotsky (1978) sees learning as taking place with others, and he views the transition between the two planes as a dialogic process in the 'zone of proximal development' described as:

> The distance between the actual developmental level as determined by independent problem solving and the level of potential development as determined through problem solving under adult guidance or in collaboration with more capable peers. (p. 86)

This notion of learning as taking place not just through dialogue, but particularly through dialogue with 'experts' – whether adults or more 'capable' peers – is central to Vygotsky. Modern researchers have further enlarged and refined this notion.

The defining property of human mental action is the fact that it is mediated by culturally constructed artifacts, according to Vygotsky. These include not only technical tools but also psychological tools such as algebraic symbols, signs, and more elaborated sign systems such as language. As Lantolf and Appel (1994b) explain, Vygotsky principally claims that, just as they use technical tools for manipulating their environment, people use psychological tools for directing and controlling their physical and mental behavior. Signs carry a fundamental importance in that they are internally oriented at the subject of activity; that is, they are directed at causing changes in the behavior of others or oneself.

In sum, Vygotsky sees mind as socially constituted through the appropriation and transformation of social interactions and through mediation via semiotic systems, in particular language (Forman *et al.*, 1993; Rodby, 1992). He considers mediation an active process and also emphasizes that the introduction of a new cultural tool into this active process transforms it. For him, the explanation of consciousness lies in the interactions linking humans to each other and to their artifacts (Lantolf & Appel, 1994b).

Contemporary Sociocultural Perspectives

Derivatives of Vygotskian and Bakhtinian theories form the basis of contemporary work in a variety of disciplines, including psychology, anthropology, and anthropological linguistics (Cole, 1996; Goodwin, 1990; Miller & Goodnow, 1995; Ochs, 1988, 1991; Rogoff, 1990, 1994; Schieffelin &

Ochs, 1986; Wertsch, 1991). Following Vygotsky and Bakhtin, current sociocultural theorists see learning as located in social interactional processes. Specifically, they view language socialization as a process which results in the acquisition of linguistic and social knowledge and skills through language practices and through interaction with more expert or more knowledgeable others in order to become competent members of a social group (Lave & Wenger, 1991; Ochs, 1988, 1991; Rogoff, 1990; Schieffelin & Ochs, 1986; Wenger, 1998).

Vygotsky's notion that learning, meaning, or even consciousness derive from human interaction requires a unit of analysis beyond the individual. Vygotsky's follower Leontiev proposed such a unit in his notion of activity. As Donato and McCormick (1994) explain, activity can be described in terms of sociocultural settings involving collaborative interaction, intersubjectivity, and assisted performance. They also summarize the notion more simply as 'the who, what, when, where, and why, the small recurrent dramas of everyday life, played on the stage of home, school, community, and workplace' (p. 455). Contemporary sociocultural theorists have grappled further with developing a unit of analysis that conceptualizes the relationship between mental functioning and sociocultural setting. Cole (1995) reviews various recent formulations and identifies three basic similarities: an emphasis on the dialectal character of human relations; a focus on experience in the world; and a view of cognition as distributed, that is, as 'stretched across mind, body, activity, and setting' (p. 116).

Contemporary researchers have developed the metaphor of scaffolding (Wood *et al.*, 1976) to capture Vygotsky's notion of the interactive processes involved between expert and novice in problem-solving tasks. Recent discussions have considered scaffolding to be a complex interpersonal process involving the following major dimensions: semiotic devices that encourage the construction and sharing of perspectives, affective dynamics of a relationship, and the social symbol value of situations and behaviors (Antón, 1999; Antón & DiCamilla, 1998; Stone, 1993). Recent discussions have also stressed the effectiveness of scaffolding not only from expert to novice but among learners with varying degrees of expertise (Donato, 1994; Swain & Lapkin, 1998; Swain, 2000; Wells, 1999).

Among contemporary sociocultural theorists, I have found the work of Lave and Wenger (1991) most useful. It emphasizes the sociopolitical aspects and conditions of possibility for learning, currently identified as an important area of research in English language learning (e.g., Lin, 1996; McGroarty, 1998; Norton Peirce, 1993; Pavlenko, 2000). Lave and Wenger's theory of *legitimate peripheral participation* focuses on the relationship between learning and situated social situations and conceptualizes the learning process as one of participation in a community of practice. This view of learning concerns the 'whole person acting in the world' and 'focuses attention on ways in which it is an evolving, continuously renewed set of relations' (Lave & Wenger, 1991: 49–50).

In this theory, knowledge is located within the community. A community of practice is described as 'a set of relations among persons, activity, and world' which exists over time and in relation with other communities (Lave & Wenger, 1991: 98). It is further described as a shared history of learning, involving relations of mutual engagement, negotiation of a joint enterprise, and the development of a shared repertoire (Wenger, 1998).

Lave and Wenger (1991) emphasize that 'the social structure of this practice, its power relations, and its conditions for legitimacy define possibilities for … legitimate peripheral participation' (p. 98). All members of any community engage in legitimate peripheral participation, an interactive process, by simultaneously performing several roles, each implying a different sort of responsibility, a different set of role relations, and a different interactive involvement. As members participate, their social relations within the community change and their understanding and knowledgeable skills develop. Through their legitimate peripherality, newcomers as well as old-timers absorb and are absorbed in the culture of practice, assembling constantly evolving viewpoints from which to understand the practice.

Lave and Wenger (1991) insist that learners must be favorably situated legitimate peripheral participants in ongoing practice in order for learning identities to be engaged and to develop into full participation. Thus, it is access to practice, rather than to instruction, as a resource for learning that is critical in their theory.

> The practice of the community creates the potential 'curriculum' in the broadest sense – that which may be learned by newcomers with legitimate peripheral access.… Learning itself is an improvised practice: A learning curriculum unfolds in opportunities for engagement in practice. It is not specified as a set of dictates for proper practice. (pp. 92–93)

Learners need access to a wide range of ongoing activity and other members of the community and to information, resources, and opportunities for participation in order to become full members of a community of practice. This can be problematic and conflictual, and it necessarily involves power relations. In this view, learning involves the construction of identities:

> Viewing learning as legitimate peripheral participation means that

learning is not merely a condition for membership, but is itself an evolving form of membership. We conceive of identities as long-term, living relations between persons and their place and participation in communities of practice. Thus identity, knowing, and social membership entail one another. (Lave & Wenger, 1991: 53)

Lave and Wenger stress that talk is a major medium for the transformation of identity in communities of practice, describing how apprentices gained a sense of belonging through personal storytelling in one apprenticeship situation they studied. They also stress that apprentices learn not only skills but norms and values, of which they never become aware, and they emphasize the reproductive aspects of a community of practice.

For Lave and Wenger (1991), learning and identity are inseparable. Through legitimate peripheral participation, an apprentice's contributions to ongoing activity gain value in practice and provide evidence for self-evaluation of effort, thus providing inherent motivation to learn. Moving toward full participation in practice involves becoming part of the community and developing a sense of identity as a master practitioner. This, Lave and Wenger acknowledge, entails changes in cultural identity and social relations.

Identity

The philosopher Taylor (1985, 1989, 1993) argues that in Western thought the individual has been conceptualized as metaphysically independent of society, obscuring the 'way in which an individual is constituted by language and culture which can only be maintained and renewed in the communities he is part of' (Taylor, 1985, cited in Wertsch, 1991: 69). These atomistic conceptions of self are quite different from the thinking of the political philosopher Marx and his followers, who assume that human nature is not essential but socially produced and changing. Vygotsky's thinking on the social nature of learning mirrors this latter assumption: 'Humans' psychological nature represents the aggregate of internalized social relations that have become functions for the individual and form the individual's structure' (Vygotsky, 1981, cited in Wertsch, 1991: 26).

In similar fashion, Bakhtin stresses that we come into being in our relations with others: 'As the human body is originally formed into the mother's womb, the individual's consciousness awakens involved into the other's consciousness' (Bakhtin, 1984a, cited in Smolka *et al.*, 1995: 181). For Bakhtin, individual consciousness is intersubjective and is realized in dialogue with others through multiple ideological encounters:

The importance of struggling with another's discourse, its influence in the history of an individual's coming to ideological consciousness, is enormous. One's own discourse and one's own voice, although born of another or dynamically stimulated by another, will sooner or later begin to liberate themselves from the authority of the other's discourse. This process is made more complex by the fact that a variety of alien voices enter into the struggle for influence within an individual's consciousness (just as they struggle with one another in surrounding social reality). (1981: 348)

Bakhtin stresses that we cannot know ourselves directly and that we must forge a self from the multiple and conflicting voices in our surroundings. This process continues throughout our lifetimes and takes place through the activity of authoring, by which we translate '"life" outside language into the patterns afforded by words, by sentences – and above all, by narratives of various kinds' (Holquist, 1990: 84).

Like Vygotsky and Bakhtin, contemporary writers working in a variety of disciplines also emphasize the socially constructed nature of the self (e.g., Hall, 1990, 1996; Holland *et al.*, 1998). Ochs (1993) draws attention to how we use language to display our identities and membership in groups. Wenger (1998) argues that identity should be seen as an ongoing process of negotiating the self, where issues of power and belonging figure centrally. He also sees identification as central, writing of how we identify not only by engaging in a community of practice but also through imagining our place within it.

Researchers working within critical and poststructural perspectives in the second language field also take a socially situated view of identity. They argue that the learner should be seen as 'a social agent, located in a network of social relations, in specific places in a social structure' (Kress, 1989: 5). For these theorists, language should be seen as a social practice taking place within relationships of power and the individual should be seen as having a complex identity, changing over time and space (Norton Peirce, 1995).

In her work on identity and second language learning, Norton (Norton Peirce, 1993, 1995; Norton, 2000) draws on the work of the French sociologist Bourdieu to emphasize the centrality of power relations to our understanding of a language learner's social identity. She defines social identity as: 'how a person understands his or her relationship to the social world, how that relationship is constructed across time and space, and how the person understands possibilities for the future' (Norton, 2000: 5). Bourdieu (1977, 1979, 1991) theorizes that we operate with an unconscious sense of our place in the social spaces in which we interact. This embodied under-standing manifests itself in such phenomena as our bearing and gestures, the interactional time we appropriate, and our manner in doing so. Bourdieu emphasizes that speakers' ability to 'command a listener' is unequally distributed because of the symbolic power relations among speakers. He argues that when they speak, people wish not only to be understood but to be 'believed, obeyed, respected, distinguished' (Bourdieu, 1977: 648). He warns us that we orient our speech not so much according to linguistic expectations but rather by our chances of reception. He proposes that the notion of competence should be expanded to include an awareness of 'the right to speech' or in his words, 'the power to impose reception' (1977: 648).

In addition to Bourdieu, Norton draws on the feminist poststructuralist theorist, Weedon, to reconceptualize the relation between the individual and the social in learning. Weedon (1987) defines subjectivity as 'the conscious and unconscious thoughts and emotions of the individual, her sense of herself and her ways of understanding her relation to the world' (p. 32). This view conceptualizes subjectivity as complex and multiple, a site of struggle, and changing over time.

Norton challenges current notions of motivation in second language learning, and places questions of access and power relations at the center of understanding a person's choices and desires. Instead of the more limited concept of motivation, Norton proposes the notion of investment, which 'signals the socially and historically constructed relationship of learners to the target language' (Norton, 2000: 10). She links this notion to Bourdieu's critical perspective, explaining, 'If learners invest in a second language, they do so with the understanding that they will acquire a wider range of symbolic and material resources, which will in turn increase the value of their cultural capital. Learners expect or hope to have a good return on their investment – a return that will give them access to hitherto unattainable resources' (p. 10). Norton empasizes that her notion of investment conceives of the language learner as having a complex social history and multiple desires. It presupposes that, when they speak, language learners constantly organize and reorganize a sense of who they are and how they relate to the social world. For Norton, an 'investment' in the target language is also an investment in a learner's own social identity, an identity that is constantly changing across time and space (p. 11).

Price (1996) argues that Norton takes too rational a view of the person and hence falls into contradiction with the radical contingency of personal identity, interests, and desires inherent in poststructuralist thought. In the latter view, we are positioned in multiple and often conflicting discourses in our everyday interactions and we actively position ourselves when we speak, often shifting discourses to position ourselves more powerfully. If research focused on a more contingent personhood, according to Price, it would shift its emphasis from examining 'the ways in which learners might come to exercise the right to speak and develop competence to realize individually given and sustained pre-given interests' to examining 'how interests and discourse positions are structured and taken up by learners in ever changing contexts' (Price, 1996: 336).

In her research on young second language learners in Great Britain, Bourne (1992) argues for a similar shift of emphasis, saying also that we need to understand that unconscious and powerful drives work themselves out in how we take up positions available within different discourses. For Bourne, the work of the feminist theorist Kristeva is important in recognizing that unconscious and unarticulated drives operate in discursive practices, which she terms 'desire.' For Kristeva, the person is not simply rationalist but split between the conscious and unconscious, and the drives of the human organism are organized through the regulation of social practices (Bourne, 1992: 441).

These arguments echo those of researchers who claim that implicitly rationalist views underlie much contemporary work on identity and the self (Henriques *et al.*, 1984). Following Foucault, they argue that when we take on discursive positions, we also take on the psychic and emotional structure implicit in them. In their view, we need to include a psychoanalytic perspective in any account of subjectivity and to address the specificity of the construction of actual subjectivities in the domain of discursive practices in order to overcome problems associated with the implicit notion of the rational pre-given personality.

More recently, Walkerdine (1997) has criticized situated learning researchers for maintaining an undertheorized notion of the person. She emphasizes that we must try to understand the complexity of the process by which our subjectivities are formed. For her, this requires a consideration of contemporary psychoanalytic theory, which deals with affect and the unconscious.

Arguing against traditional psychology's separation of affect from cognition, the critical psychologist Litowitz (1993, 1997) also draws on contemporary psychoanalytic theory to address motivational dynamics in learning. Litowitz (1997) places questions of identification (and resistance) at the heart of learning and motivation. She defines identification as the psychological process whereby the person assimilates an aspect, property, or attribute of the other and is transformed, wholly or partially, after the model the other provides. And she extends this notion with recent formulations by the twentieth century psychoanalytic theorist, Lacan (1977), in which one may identify not only with the other but with the other's wants or desires (and in which one may even seek to be the desire of the other).

Lacan's theory assumes desire to be the motivating principle of human life, and the 'other' is the position of control of desire and meaning.[2] Litowitz (1993) hypothesizes that the desire to be the adult or to be the one whom the adult wants him to be is what motivates a child to master a task. Drawing a parallel with Vygotsky's (1986) 'inner speech' (socialized speech turned inwards), she summarizes her views on the interconnections between learning and identification as follows:

> We may say that, as our inner speech is the internalized speech of others, our self is constituted by the internalized others who speak. Our selves are created out of these identifications with others, with social groups, and their desires. Their desires become ours; and we become their desires. Whether we agree or refuse to teach or learn has its source at this level of psychological analysis. (p. 189)

All this work on socially constructed identity falls within the context of the contemporary sociocultural perspectives I have outlined. Here, as in the second language field, researchers have struggled with well-entrenched notions of a unitary individual divorced from social context. They call for the need to study situated learners in their interpersonal relationships with one another (Minick *et al.*, 1993). More recently, they argue that we need to probe further into bodily lived experience, affect and the unconscious, and meaning-making processes (Kirshner & Whitson, 1997). As Kirshner and Whitson state:

> The notion of the individual ... needs to be fundamentally reformulated.... This reformulation probes the physiological, psychoanalytic, and semiotic constitution of persons. (1997: 9)

Ethnographic Research

In a recent article, Davis (1995) contrasts two research traditions, which until recently appear to have operated independently from one another in second language education: second language acquisition research on the one hand, and linguistic anthropology and the ethnography of communication on the other. Second language acquisition researchers aim at finding regularities that one can describe and predict universally, and they tend to rely on positivist, psychological research models preferring statistical analyses and experimental and quasi-experimental research designs (Ellis,

1985, 1994; Larsen-Freeman & Long, 1991). Linguistic anthropologists and ethnographers of communication see human relationships, social contexts, and situations as primary in language learning; these scholars use and rely on ethnographic approaches in order to gain in-depth understandings of the complexity and particularity of learning (e.g., Ortiz, 1988; Saravia-Shore & Arvizu, 1992; Trueba *et al.*, 1981).

Ethnography, as Duff (1995) explains, provides 'a holistic, grounded, and participant-informed perspective of schooling, either in general terms or with respect to particular activities through what Geertz (1973) calls a *thick description* of cultural contexts' (p. 507). It is linked with a view of language learning as a matter of language socialization rather than acquisition (Watson-Gegeo, 1988). This perspective sees language and cultural learning as interdependent and focuses on how learners acquire linguistic and social knowledge (such as values, attitudes, roles, identities, and emotional stances) by participating in a community's communicative practices. Researchers focus on how this knowledge is dynamically co-constructed by community members in their ongoing interactions. Some researchers also draw on critical and poststructural theories to illuminate the discursive and political nature of classroom practices and their multiplicity and contradictions.

Ethnographic research attempts to combine two perspectives: the participants' 'emic' view and the 'etic,' outside view of the supposedly objective observer. Geertz describes the dialectal tension that operates between the emic and etic perspectives in the following way:

> Confinement to experience-near concepts leaves an ethnographer awash in immediacies, as well as entangled in vernacular. Confinement to experience-distant ones leaves him stranded in abstractions and smothered in jargon. The real question ... is what roles the two sorts of concepts play in anthropological analysis ... so as to produce an interpretation of the way a people lives which is neither imprisoned within their mental horizons, ... nor systematically deaf to the distinctive tonalities of their existence, ... (Geertz, 1976: 223)

A critical consideration for ethnographic research is the establishment of research credibility (Davis, 1992, 1995). Among the most important measures of credibility are prolonged engagement and persistent observation; 'thick description,' which enables the reader to 'become a coanalyst of the data and interpretations presented' (Davis, 1995: 448); and triangulation, using multiple perspectives, data or methods to check observations and interpretations (Hammersley & Atkinson, 1983; Lincoln & Guba, 1985).

Recent Ethnographic Studies

Recent years have seen a growing number of ethnographic studies focusing on language socialization in classrooms involving English and other language learners. These include long-term studies of young English language learners integrated in mainstream elementary school classrooms in Great Britain (Blackledge, 2000; Bourne, 1992), Canada (Hunter, 1997; Toohey, 2000) and the United States (Gutierrez, 1994; Platt & Troudi, 1997; Vasquez *et al.*, 1994; Willett, 1995), as well as studies of older learners in secondary school, university, or adult 'ESL' classes (e.g., Duff, 1995; Gutierrez *et al.*, 1995; Haneda, 1997; Lin, 1996, 1999; McKay & Wong, 1996; Miller, 1999, 2000; Norton, 2000; Poole, 1992; Rymes, 1997; Siegal, 1996).

In elementary school, Platt and Troudi (1997) examine the classroom participation of Mary, a Grebo-speaking child from Liberia, who was mainstreamed in a Grade 3 classroom in the south-eastern United States, from the perspective of sociocultural theory. The researchers report that, although she quickly learned functional communication skills by participating in the classroom community, in most academic situations Mary developed 'coping behaviors' which only superficially suggested participation and consumed much time which she could have spent more effectively with adult monitoring and assistance. They argue that sociocultural theory can powerfully inform the teaching of minority language children because it views linguistic and cognitive development as interrelated and encourages close monitoring and working within children's 'zone of proximal development' (Vygotsky, 1978). Haneda (1997) places a similar emphasis on the zone of proximal development as an important construct for second language classrooms in her study of a classroom of adult Canadian university students learning Japanese.

Reporting on an ethnographic study of the effects of writing process instruction on elementary school-aged Latino children in the western United States, Gutierrez (1994) shows how the contexts for learning to write were constructed differently, both dynamically and socially, in three classrooms and how these differences in context led to differential access to learning. She identifies three different scripts evident in the classrooms: recitation, responsive, and responsive/collaborative. She reports that students only had the opportunity to take up a broad range of interactional and conversational roles and relationships that helped them construct extended texts in the responsive/collaborative classroom, where the bounds between teacher and students were more fluid and where both actively co-managed the discourse and interaction.

Related to the question of access, Lin's (1996) ethnographic study of

English language lessons in eight Hong Kong secondary school classrooms analyzes how the various teachers used different varieties of discourse formats to organize different types of lesson activities for their students and how these formats provide differential access to linguistic and cultural resources. Drawing on data from four of the classrooms, Lin (1999) focuses her analysis on whether teachers and students co-constructed English lessons in such a way that they could reproduce or transform the students' social worlds.

Willett (1995) reports on a year-long study of four English language learners (three girls and one boy) who were mainstreamed in a Grade 1 elementary school classroom in the north-eastern United States. She shows how the micropolitics of gender and class mediated the children's access to language and opportunities to develop their competence in English in the setting she studied. The three girl students, who were allowed to sit together over the year, appropriated interactional routines and strategies and could display their competence and gain identities as good students by cooperating and mutually supporting one another. In contrast, the boy student, Xavier, placed between two English-speaking girls who tended not to help him because he was a boy, had to rely more frequently on help from adults and began to be seen as a needy child who could not work independently, an identity which was then reinforced by ethnic and class stereotypes. Willett stresses the need to study the complex particularity of learning settings; in her words, 'the sociocultural ecology of the community, school, and classroom shaped the kinds of microinteractions that occurred and thus the nature of their language learning over the course of the year' (p. 473).

The role of schools in reproducing inequitable relations of power operating in the broader society is taken up by Blackledge (2000) in her study of 18 Bangladeshi families and their six-year-old children conducted in an urban setting in Great Britain. Although she documents a range of home literacy practices and active support for Bengali literacy on the part of the children's mothers, she reports little recognition or value placed on these in the school. In addition, she shows that although the mothers viewed themselves as competent, they were constructed by teachers as inadequate contributors to their children's literacy learning and their participation in their children's schooling was marginalized. Blackledge argues that the schools' right to define what constitutes literacy and their limitation and neglect of home literacies reflect a coercive exercise of power which must be reversed by building on the linguistic and cultural resources of families.

Bourne (1992) conducted a year-long ethnographic study of a multilingual primary classroom of English-, Bengali- and Cantonese-speaking children in Great Britain. Drawing from a range of critical theories which emphasize the social construction of students in schools, she shows how students were positioned in relation to teachers' beliefs and how discursive practices worked to construct a particular form of shared knowledge and a particular ideal student, and the implications of this for the English language learners she studied. They were either isolated or placed with other beginners upon entry to the classroom, a situation which restricted access to the teacher and to other students and seemed to lead to more permanent isolation and low status over the course of the year. Bourne also examines peer interactions and shows how children actively positioned themselves in the variety of discourses operating in the classroom. She stresses the need for viewing the classroom as a complex heteroglossic site and for reconceptualizing the notion of the individual in accordance with a poststructuralist theoretical framework.

Drawing from a two-year ethnographic study of language development in Grades 4 and 5 multicultural urban classrooms in eastern Canada, Hunter (1997) uses poststructural theory to analyze the multiple and often contradictory positioning of one pupil, Roberto, a Portuguese- and English-speaking bilingual child, in writing activities in the two grades. She shows how identity in relation to school expectations can conflict with identities among peers and how children's negotiations of these conflicts can bear on their second language and literacy learning. Hunter calls attention to the multiple, shifting and conflicting identities of English language learners and stresses the complexity of students' investments in contrast to the school's construction of the students' identities based on ethnicity and language proficiency.

McKay and Wong (1996) make similar points in their two-year ethnographic study of four Mandarin-speaking immigrant students in Grades 7 and 8 in a California public school. They identify five distinct but mutually interacting discourses in which the students were positioned in their English language classes and show how these discourses helped shape the investments each student made toward learning English. They also trace how students actively negotiated their identities and exercised agency by repositioning themselves, resisting positioning, and setting up counter-discourses. In their conclusions, the researchers stress that agency enhancement and identity enhancement seemed to be paramount considerations for their students, in contrast to Norton's emphasis on investment enhancement.

As discussed in Chapter 1, Toohey (2000) investigated identity practices in her longitudinal ethnographic study following six English language learners in a Canadian elementary school from kindergarten through Grade 2. In kindergarten, Toohey analyzes how the identities of the six children were differentially constructed along various dimensions of competence (i.e., academic, physical, behavioral, social and linguistic). She places her analysis of identity in relation to classroom ranking and normalizing practices, showing how three of the English language learners (Harvey, Martin, and Surjeet) became constructed as deficient language learners, while the others were more favorably positioned. In addition, she critiques the notion of 'ESL' as a construct produced by practices, in her words 'a position, not an essence' (Toohey, 2000: 76).

Toohey analyzes how three classroom practices in Grade 1 (sitting in your own desk, using your own things, and using your own ideas) contributed to individualizing the children and stratifying the community, with a resulting negative impact for some of the English language learners in terms of classroom participation and identity construction. She also analyzes three discursive practices in Grade 2 (whole group discussions, teacher-mandated partner and small group conversations and student-managed conversations), detailing how these facilitated or limited children's access to appropriating classroom language. She identifies desirable and powerful identity positions, access to peer expertise, and opportunities to play in language as critical for children's appropriation of language.

Toohey's work on classroom practices shows how these practices 'establish social relations that determine access to classroom resources and ultimately to learning' (2000: 3). Her work on identity points to the need for further detailed information on how children take up and/or resist identity positions in their day-to-day interactions.

The Present Study

In this study, I closely examine the experiences of one kindergarten child and provide detailed information on social relations and identity positions that I hope will complement Toohey's work.

In my work, I join a growing number of researchers (e.g., Gutierrez, 1993; Gutierrez *et al.*, 1995; Hall, 1995; Lin, 1996; Norton, 2000; Toohey, 1996, 1998, 2000; Willett, 1995; Willett *et al.*, 1999) who ground their work in contemporary approaches that characteristically emphasize the situated character of human understanding and communication, a broad view of human agency, and the integration in practice of agent, world, and activity (Lave & Wenger, 1991).

McGroarty clearly stated the value and urgency of such work in a recent issue of *Language Learning*:

Research both within applied linguistics and across a range of related social sciences suggests that, until linguists develop better means of describing the interrelationships between the individual and group psychosocial, cognitive, and linguistic aspects of language acquisition and teaching and the opportunities and constraints of the social contexts surrounding language acquisition and development, they cannot hope to address the most intellectually challenging and practically significant aspects of language learning and teaching. (1998: 592)

McGroarty challenges applied linguists to rethink the boundaries of their work to identify and incorporate more precisely and comprehensively the subjective and social dimensions of language learning along with linguistic aspects. She reviews how contemporary scholarship conducted outside of the prevalent SLA paradigm has contributed to our understanding of language learning in the following three areas: identity; optimal environments for language learning; and institutional constraints affecting language learning and instruction. She further identifies these areas as 'the next horizons' for applied linguistics research.

My work lies within the research traditions McGroarty mentions, which have arisen in disciplinary and cross-disciplinary areas in anthropology, psychology, linguistics, sociolinguistics, and sociology (Cole *et al.*, 1997; Duranti & Goodwin, 1992; Goodnow, 1990a, 1990b; Hanks, 1996; Holland *et al.*, 1998; Miller & Goodnow, 1995; Ochs, 1988; Wertsch, 1991). In it, I address issues of identity and access, two of the key areas identified by McGroarty.

The theoretical perspectives I use include Bakhtin's (1981, 1984a, 1984b, 1986) and Vygotsky's (1978, 1986) theories on language and learning, the work of contemporary sociocultural theorists on situated learning (Lave & Wenger, 1991), and poststructural theories on identity (Henriques *et al.*, 1984; Norton, 1997a, 1997b, 2000; Norton Peirce, 1995; Weedon, 1987). These theoretical perspectives hold the underlying assumption that there is an interdependence between the agent and his or her sociohistorical environment.

In order to provide a richness of both individual and contextual data, I decided on an ethnographic study of one English language learner enrolled in a mainstream kindergarten classroom in an urban area of British Columbia. In this work, I follow one child, Hari, over the course of his kindergarten year and show how he experiences different possibilities for learning with different people and with the same people at different times. My investigation centers on the following question:

What are the social and political dimensions of Hari's relationships with his classmates and teacher and how do these affect possibilities for learning?

I turn now to an account of how I conducted the study.

Notes

1. Following Hall (1997) and Lantolf (2000), I use the qualifier 'mainstream' to refer to the dominant strand of second language acquisition research, which is based on a cognitive model. In the discussion, I am concerned with the central orientation of this research and thus simplify the rich and varied approaches that can be found (for reviews, see Ellis, 1994; Mitchell & Myles, 1998).
2. Lacan hypothesizes that the infant's recognition of herself in the mirror at about six months provides the first experience of the self as object, the sense of self. This experience is imaginary or illusory, because the infant cannot really distinguish between the self and the mirror image. Through the experience of seeing the self as object, Lacan hypothesizes, the infant comes into a position to both want the mother, to control her and hence satisfaction, and to want to be what the mother wants. The relation is a narcissistic one and it is in this 'mirror stage' that the process of establishing desire for the 'other' begins (Urwin, 1984).

Chapter 3
Methodology

> … close observation of individual differences can be as powerful a method in science as the quantification of predictable behavior in a zillion identical atoms …
>
> (Gould, 1987, cited in Tannen, 1989: 35)

The site for the study was an elementary school in a working-class neighborhood in a large suburb close to Vancouver, British Columbia (see Toohey, 2000 and Day, 1999 for full details of the research site). In the school in which we worked, kindergarten children whose first language is not English are offered a Language Development program, an additional kindergarten session running in the afternoons; participation is voluntary. Qualification for the program is determined through an assessment procedure administered by the classroom teacher at the beginning of the year to all children whose home language is not English (as indicated by a parent questionnaire).

At the beginning of the Cohort 2 study, the teacher (Mrs Clark) provided us with a list of the children identified as qualifying for this Language program. In all, seven children (one boy, six girls) from a classroom of 19 children (nine boys, ten girls) were eligible: three Polish and three Punjabi-speaking children and one Spanish-speaking child.[1] Two families declined to participate, one because of objection to the video recording and the other out of lack of interest. Five families agreed to participate in the study. Of the five children in the sample, three (Hari, Manjit, and Raj) are Punjabi-speaking, and two (Claudia and Paula) are Polish-speaking. Hari is the only boy.

Data Collection

I observed the five focal children over the entire school year from mid-September 1996 to mid-June 1997. I observed them in the morning kindergarten session once a week and in their afternoon Language program session once monthly. I tried to keep a low profile in the classroom, taking a stance similar to Dyson's (1997) in her classroom research: a 'curious, rather ignorant but very nonthreatening person, who wished to witness their goings on' (p. 25).

I kept running field notes of my observations, noted contextual information, described what the children were doing and who they were with, and wrote down interactions and speakers. For the audiotaping, I used an ambient microphone during the entire observation to capture classroom lessons, table talk, and activity time. I also used two individual microphones, trying to rotate these on the sample of five children where appropriate. Hari, the main focus of this study, declined the individual mike early in the year, seeming to view it as an encumbrance. I offered it to him again on occasion over the year, taking care not to press him; he sometimes declined and sometimes accepted.[2]

In addition, a trained video technician from Simon Fraser University, Linda Hof, videotaped the classroom for about 1½ hours once a month, beginning in November. Linda, who has a great deal of videotaping experience in classrooms and who had videotaped the children in Cohort 1 in previous years, filmed a range of instructional and non-instructional activities in which children were engaged.

During the observations, I collected documents including pedagogical materials, curriculum documents, information letters to parents, and student materials. I requested registration information, results of language assessments, and student report cards from the teacher to complete the data set.

I also interviewed the classroom teacher formally three times in the year. The interviews took place in November, early March, and June (after each reporting period) and lasted approximately 1½ hours. I used an unstructured interview format based on discussion of three broad categories: the social, academic, and linguistic progress of each child. At the end of two of the interviews, I also introduced questions regarding the teacher's goals, the curriculum, the afternoon Language program, and the classroom in general.

During my observations, I was able to discuss pertinent matters with the teacher as they came up during class time or immediately after class. The teacher had a very demanding teaching schedule, however, and time was limited.

Parents were interviewed at home near the beginning and end of the school year. The interviews were conducted in the home language by bilingual researchers (Bozena Karwowska and Kunwal Aurora for the Polish and Punjabi-speaking families, respectively). These bilingual researchers also interviewed the children at this time in their first language (L1) in order to keep a record of the children's use of their home language. They brought their own L1 materials and also used pilot instruments that we developed to build conversations with the children.[3] The researchers audiotaped family interviews and took notes where appropriate. After interviewing the families, they reviewed all the material they had collected and wrote written summaries of their experiences; I also debriefed them and discussed their summaries. I profited in this aspect of the work from my experience in a research project on multilingual families on which I had collaborated (Dagenais & Day, 1998, 1999).

I adapted transcription conventions from Ochs (1996) to transcribe the recordings used in this work, keeping these at a minimum to ensure readability. Trained research assistants (Lisa Day and Barbara Muthwa-Kuehn) assisted me in the work of transcribing. The conventions I used are provided in the Appendix.

Analysis

Consistent with ethnographic methodology, I analyzed the data in an ongoing fashion throughout the data collection period and afterwards, as I reflected, refined perceptions, and gained further insights as the study progressed (cf. Lincoln & Guba, 1985; Ramanathan & Atkinson, 1999). Though the manner in which I have laid out the theoretical basis for this work might suggest that I imposed theory in a top-down fashion, this was far from the case. I conducted some ongoing reading of the literature during the observation period. This process of concurrent theoretical research was intensified after the observations were completed, during data analysis and writing.

After I had collected the data and assembled the data set, I read all the case material several times, noting observations, hypotheses, and critical incidents, making summaries of my interpretations, and tagging features of the data I considered important. Merriam (1988) describes this aspect of the research as 'holding a conversation with the data' (p. 131). I also did some preliminary coding of the material. These codes included categories such as participant structures, seating arrangements, code-switching, and repetition, for example.

I also started to construct case profiles for each child, as one way of approaching the data. To do this, I reviewed all the data for each child several times, including notes, observations, classroom recording, and interview transcriptions. As I did this, I made notes and tagged the data for each child in binders, using color-coded tags. I then began to construct the case profiles. During this time, I also developed a conference paper proposal on the topic of repetition, as this seemed a salient aspect of the data collected. Because I found Hari's data particularly interesting in this regard, I decided to complete the case profile for Hari. After finishing the conference paper (Day, 1998), I decided to use a case study approach and focus on Hari. I wanted to pursue some of the findings from the conference paper further, had some hunches about other aspects of the data which I thought were promising, and felt that Hari's case would add different information and present useful contrasts with some of the children discussed by Toohey (1996). The considerable investment of work and time that I had made in completing the case profile and conference paper also weighed in my decision.

The case profile I initially constructed constituted one layer of analysis, and a useful starting point. It helped me begin to understand the data, formulate hypotheses, and delve into some of the theoretical literature with respect to what I was seeing. Most useful, however, I returned to the raw data again and again, working in a recursive fashion from data to theory and back again, as I speculated, developed tentative hypotheses and interpretations, and returned to the data to check my interpretations.

I used triangulation throughout the analysis and writing (across different researchers, different methods, such as observation and interviews, and different data sources, including field notes, audiotapes, and videos). Where I found disconfirmatory evidence, I tried to reconsider the implications for my analysis and/or incorporate it into the text. I also submitted the text to the teacher for review and invited her to make comments and delete, correct and challenge material (member check). As she had participated in the study of the previous kindergarten cohort (Cohort 1), she was familiar with some of the written work from the study.

Hammersley and Atkinson (1983) emphasize that the researcher is the research instrument par excellence and stress the need for reflexivity in all phases of the research. Over the course of the project, I kept a journal in which I detailed in an ongoing manner my personal thoughts and reactions after the observations. This journal was valuable to me throughout the year, especially in the beginning months of the project. Because of my childhood background, I found that I identified completely with the children we were studying; after each observation I wondered whether I (or any of my friends from my own ethnic background) had walked in their shoes. I tried carefully not to project my own experiences onto those of the children nor to interpret data based on my own personal experiences. Personal journal writing helped me understand my own preoccupations and thus was an important part of the research process.

Lincoln and Guba (1985) recommend debriefings by peers to guard against researcher bias. In this study, three different researchers were involved in the observations; we met periodically and also communicated electronically to discuss various aspects of the study and share readings and stories from the field. All of this is important from the point of view of the research: to express concerns, issues, ideas, and hunches and to triangulate and challenge one another. It is also important from the personal point of view: for emotional support and for building rapport and a sense of community. I was also able to discuss various aspects of the study with research colleagues who were not involved in the study, though this was not a systematic procedure of the study.

By way of a final note on this section, I would like to mention that my granddaughter, who is a year younger than the children I observed, was living in our home over the period of observation and data analysis. This allowed me to reflect on my work in the light of living experiences and reflections on a child of similar age.

Ethics and Power Relations

Contemporary research perspectives (e.g., Graue & Walsh, 1998; Skeggs, 1995) urge us to reflect on power relations and consider the important question of ethics in conducting research. I am mindful that I write from the privileged position of university-based researcher and that I gain personal and professional benefit from the study. Throughout the study I tried to maintain warm and collegial relations with the teacher, Mrs Clark. On the days of my visits, I would generally eat lunch in the staff room with her, the other kindergarten teacher, and a few of the staff members, and engage in general conversation with them. I think that this helped increase familiarity. I also profited from the relations that had been built up with the teacher during the research on the Cohort 1 project.

Once in late April, I returned to class after having missed the previous week's observation. Mrs Clark greeted me with the news that 22 of the chicks that had been incubating in the classroom had hatched, telling me that she kept on hoping that I would come back to see them hatching and that each day she would wonder whether I would come, wishing I was there (FN 5/6/97: 12). In my journal notes for that day, I reflect on this:

> Drats! away just at the wrong time. What one gains in being away for a while, perspective, one loses in the intimate sharing of daily events. I reflect on how much Mrs Clark's saying 'I wish you were here' meant to me.… Intimacy, I am in a certain way part of the class.

Two incidents suggest that our relations were warm but that the underlying purposes of my being there were not forgotten. One time close to

Valentine's Day, I noticed a Valentine card saying 'Hot stuff' posted among those on the classroom door. Mrs Clark greeted me as she was circulating in the classroom; when she did, I could not help replying to her with a joking reference to 'Hot Stuff.' Mrs Clark laughed, put her hands on my shoulders and hugged me quickly from the back, saying, 'But you know better, right!' (FN 2/13/97: 2–3). Another time I joked with her about her upcoming birthday as I said goodbye to her at the end of the year, and she in turn answered jokingly, 'Good-by, Miss PhD!' (Journal, 6/97).

Skeggs (1995) urges us to consider how we can reciprocate, care and be honest, and not exploit. As one way of reciprocating, we developed and piloted an oral assessment procedure which could be used to complement the assessment instrument used for the Language program. We also scheduled a separate video session to film the various kindergarten stations and offered to assist the two kindergarten teachers in preparing a demonstration video to show to prospective kindergarten parents.

In addition to ethical considerations with the teacher were those with the children (Graue & Walsh, 1998); questions of power relations are obvious here. I came to the classroom weekly, hoping to be as unobtrusive as possible, smiling at the children and talking to them when they talked to me. I often got down amongst them to do the observing. I tried to take note of my interactions with the children in my field notes and reflect on these afterwards.

Though power relations between adults and children are unequal, I wonder how important our presence in the class actually was to the children. Manjit dramatically showed me one day how little we might mean. She tapped me persistently, saying 'I got to show you something,' and then completely forgot me when she was distracted by one of her classmates. As my notes put it, 'I have been ditched! Manjit said she was going to show me something and completely forgot about it' (FN 3/4/97: 3). However, it is important to be aware that the children have a subsidiary awareness of what is going on in the room and that as observers, we are part of what is going on. Indeed, it is perfectly possible that my presence as an observer helped create 'research data,' as an incident in the next chapter will illustrate.

Notes

1. In addition, two others who arrived later in the year qualified for the Language program: an Arabic-speaking girl (Nadia) who came in December and a Punjabi-speaking boy (Rajinder) who came in May. Because of their later arrival, their participation in the study was not solicited.
2. In her study of a Grade 1 classroom, Willett (1995) reports that she was unable to individually record a male English language learner she was observing. Ac-

cording to Willett, none of the boys would wear the individual recorder because the girls in her study had labeled it as their 'ET baby.' There did not seem to be any strong indication in my data that there were gender differences in how the children perceived either the individual or ambient mikes I used. I should note, however, that one time I heard one boy asking another of the ambient mike on the table, 'Why do they want to tape us even?' and then engaging him in scatological language (Transcript, 1/23/97). The use of scatological language with the mike was also once noted with a girl from the afternoon class (FN 4/9/97). Neither of these children were focal children.

3. This was a three-part oral elicitation procedure using puppets and based around a puzzle. The child was invited to do the puzzle and then asked to name the people and objects, tell the puppet about the actions, and retell the story depicted in the puzzle. We developed this instrument for the teacher to use on an experimental basis and piloted it with ten children (including all the sample children) in English in the kindergarten classroom.

Chapter 4

Hari: His School, Teacher and Classroom and Language at Home and at School

No sociocultural environment exists or has identity independent of the way human beings seize meanings and resources from it, while every human being has her or his subjectivity and mental life altered through the process of seizing meanings and resources from some sociocultural environment and using them.

(Shweder, 1984, cited in Cole, 1996: 102–103)

Hari, aged five at the time the study began (September, 1996), lives in an extended family, including his parents, younger sister, grandparents, and a great-grandfather. His parents and theirs are from a village in the Punjab. At the time of the study, Hari's parents had been in Canada for eight years and they lived in a rapidly growing suburb close to Vancouver. Hari's mother completed Grade 10 and did two years of college in India, and his father did one year of a Masters degree in Economics there. They both work in the service industry, his father as a taxi driver and his mother as a cook in a chain restaurant. Hari's parents report that Punjabi is their first language and that they speak, read, and write both Punjabi and Hindi. They also report that Punjabi is the language they speak in their home but that they feel at ease speaking English in their work and daily life outside the home.

Hari's grandparents care for him while his parents are at work. His grandmother takes him to and from school; because she speaks little English, he sometimes serves as interpreter between her and the teacher. Hari's grandfather, described by the home interviewer as 'quite well educated,' reads him the English library books he brings home from school. He also teaches Hari about Sikh religion and Punjabi culture and tradition. The family all go to temple regularly and attend other cultural functions and events. In the year before Hari entered kindergarten, they had gone to India to attend a family wedding and spent over three months there.

Hari's parents consider it extremely important that he retain his home language so that he can communicate with his grandparents and other relatives and keep strong ties with his culture and religion. In the first home interview, conducted in October 1996, Hari's parents reported that he speaks Punjabi at home but can also speak and understand English.

Before entering public school, Hari attended an English pre-school for three to four months, an experience which his parents feel helped him with English and equipped him with some vocabulary. His parents report that he tends to be shy in the company of strangers or visitors but is outgoing with his cousins, aunts, and uncles. There are very few children in the neighborhood, they report, and so he does not have many friends. In addition, they discourage him from going outside because of an incident involving swearing and name-calling which occurred among some Canadian friends he once had. And so, they say, Hari spends most of his time indoors; he likes to watch Punjabi, and occasionally Hindi, movies and listen to English music on the radio.

Hari's Community and School

Hari goes to school in a mainstream kindergarten classroom in the suburb in which he lives. The suburb's population numbers approximately 300,000, spanning a wide socio-economic range. The school-age population comprises approximately 53,000 students. Over one-quarter (28%) of the general student population speak a language other than English in the home; Punjabi is the home language of more than two-fifths (42%) of these. Among the approximately 85 other languages besides Punjabi, those most widely spoken are Hindi, Chinese, Tagalog, Korean, Spanish, Vietnamese, and Polish.

The neighborhood surrounding Hari's school consists of small, lower-middle- and working-class single family residences and a rent-controlled townhouse complex. Toohey (2000) describes it as working class, on the basis of family income and education levels gleaned from census information.

The school has an enrollment of nearly 400 students, about one half of whom come from homes where languages other than English are spoken (Cantonese, French, Hindi, Polish, Punjabi, Spanish, Thai, Vietnamese, and several others). As one enters the school, one sees construction-paper flags of many different nations posted in the stairwell. Other displays reflecting the school's linguistically and culturally diverse population are not readily apparent in the corridors or other public areas. The school is more than 40 years old and is overcrowded, with about seven classes held in portables.[1] Some classrooms are small, while others, like Hari's classroom, are quite spacious.

Hari's school holds an additional kindergarten session termed the

Language Development program, for children whose first language is a language other than English. Seven children from Hari's class and 11 children from the other kindergarten class which runs concurrently with Hari's qualified for this program at the beginning of the year. The children from the latter class join Mrs Clark's children at the end of the morning for a supervised lunch period; they then attend the afternoon Language session, over which Hari's teacher, Mrs Clark, presides in her classroom.

Hari's Teacher

Mrs Clark, a native speaker of English, had been teaching for 16 years at the time this study began. She had taught kindergarten in this particular school for four years, during one of which she had also taught the Language program. Mrs Clark states that her goal is to have students who are happy and enthusiastic about learning. The mother of two children herself, she calls this her 'motherhood thing,' suggesting that she considers this her personal domain as opposed to the more formal goals in Ministry of Education documents. As she once explained:

> My whole motherhood thing for the year is that I want them to be happy, I want them to be enthusiastic toward learning, I want to turn them on to learning.... Then I have goals ... we have a document from the Ministry, so we have wide-range goals. And I have specific goals that I do in my kindergarten program, things that I want to accomplish and then I break it down into term 1, term 2, and term 3. (Teacher interview, 6/9/97)

She also has a wide range of institutional and curricular goals, carefully planned for the different terms of the year. The most important rules in her class are respect for property and for others, order, and tidiness (Teacher interview, 6/9/97).

Mrs Clark says that teaching a class with beginning English language learners is very different from teaching a linguistically more homogeneous group of children, telling me, 'I break it down more; I break down the skills.' She mentions the need to prepare carefully, monitor the children, and scaffold their work. In addition, she mentions that she repeats herself and uses more movement and gestures with songs and verses. She speaks of the careful preparation needed for teaching such classes:

> You think of it all the time. You wake up in the night thinking gee, should I have cut those out first for them, because they won't be able to (understand) where to cut. You know, today's activity in District X [referring to Elaine's district of residence, where the large majority of

students come from English-speaking homes], I would have been able to just hand it (out). Here, I had to staple a pattern piece to the black … so that as they cut out the panda bear's leg, they would cut two pieces of black underneath. It's hard to explain, but yes, I find that I have to do a lot more preparation so that we don't have a disaster. And a lot more monitoring while they're working, and showing. We do a lot more directed activities. When they open their pages and we do it step by step together, I do it either on the board or on (down) to the bottom or whatever. (Teacher interview, 11/19/96)[2]

During the time of this study, Mrs Clark was in the second year of teaching the afternoon Language program in the school. In the end-of-year interview, she acknowledges having had some initial anxieties about the class, which became dispelled by the year's end:

It's at this time of year that you start to see the rewards of the language class. You know I really do doubt the validity of it and its worth and all the rest of it in the fall when they're so tired and so cranky and you get these little pockets of Chinese and Polish and Punjabi talking their own language. I get very distressed and think how can this ever work. But now, at this time of the year, when you assess them and you get half of the ESL language class that can count beyond … the children that just get the (…), I feel sorry for those half day children (…). And they could have used a whole day program, you know, because they didn't get the ESL, because they don't speak … a second language at home, they didn't get the full day program, so I think … if some of those English-speaking parents knew that there were children in this after-noon class that had passed their little English-speaking kids, there'd be a riot. But you know, it's the way it is.…

And then, too, they just … pick up on the formal stuff, like little Kim, he's just so into letters and numbers, and he learns that kind of stuff so fast. But yet to put a sentence together grammatically correct (…), with no grammatical errors, is difficult for him.… So the formal part, a lot of them surpass the English-speaking, but … (Teacher interview, 6/9/97)

As the above transcript shows, Mrs Clark believes that the English language learners have benefited academically from having a full day at school, mentioning the progress they have made in comparison with children who attend the morning session only. She also considers learning to stay in school all day as another major benefit: 'They're really so lucky … because now they are used to that whole staying for lunch, all day stuff, whereas those other regular little guys have to go through all that adjustment in September' [when they begin Grade 1] (Teacher interview, 6/9/97). When I ask her about their English, she comments that the children have benefited linguistically: 'They've become quite verbal.... I really think the program has helped them.'

In summary, Mrs Clark sees the benefits of the afternoon class in terms of academic learning, language growth, and socialization to school. She mentions that English-speaking parents would object strenuously if they became aware of the advantages gained from the afternoon session, which was not open to their children. But in her words, 'It's the way it is.'

Hari's Classroom

Hari's class had 19 children at the beginning of the year, nine boys and ten girls. Two children (one girl, one boy) left the class, and two (one girl, one boy) joined in the first five months. In May, a Punjabi-speaking boy also joined the class.

As mentioned previously, seven children in the class (one boy, six girls) come from homes where a language other than English is spoken; they qualified for the afternoon Language Development program on the basis of a teacher assessment given at the beginning of the year. These children's home languages are Polish, Punjabi, and Spanish. Two of the newcomers, an Arabic-speaking girl who arrived in December and a Punjabi-speaking boy who arrived in May, also qualified for the Language program. The other children in Hari's class come from English-speaking homes; another language (i.e., Chinese, Hindi) is also spoken in the home of two of these children, both fluent English speakers.

Hari's kindergarten classroom is spacious and inviting. It is located on the ground floor facing the front area of the school. Another large, brightly decorated, kindergarten classroom is located across the hall. From Hari's classroom windows, one can see the front walkway to the school, part of the playground, and the busy roadway which runs beside the school. The classroom is large and easy to move around in. As a researcher, I found this advantageous, because it gave me ease of movement and different accesses to the children. Overall, the classroom appears cheerful, friendly, and comfortable.

At one end of the room lie a well-equipped playhouse and puppet-theater and a reading corner with soft cushions and many books, well-displayed and changed periodically. Mrs Clark's desk is between these centers. She sometimes sits there or stands in that area when the children come to have their work checked; however, more frequently, she works at one of the tables or circulates about the room. There are also two computer stations in her desk area. At the other end of the room lie the water center, sink, paint easels, coat rack where children store their belongings, sand table, a large locked storage cabinet, and a refrigerator.

Between the two doors (one at each end of the room) runs a long blackboard, posters, and an easel; these contain most of the material used in the daily routines. Mrs Clark usually sits or stands here for community activities such as routines (e.g., days of the week, number line, reading message), sharing, story time, giving lessons and instructions; during such times, the children sit in a circle facing her in a carpeted area. They customarily sit along the line of the circle for routines and sharing and some of the other teacher-led activities, moving within the circle when the teacher demonstrates on the easel or when she reads them a story.

There are three tables in the room where the children sit to do their craft and work activities and eat their snacks. At one end of the room, near the coat rack, is a long rectangular table accommodating about ten children; in the middle sits a smaller square table for six children; and at the other end near the playhouse stands a round table for eight children. The tables are well spaced so that the children can circulate freely, and they are close enough together so that children are not too far from one another. Children are free to choose their seating at the tables, as is the case with the circle seating also.

The classroom is decorated with the children's art projects and posters and thematic materials related to instructional themes. Much of the work is handmade by Mrs Clark rather than commercially produced, and she frequently changes it over the year. The classroom is very well equipped with resources and materials of many kinds, such as books, puzzles, puppets, blocks, dolls, a wooden train set, toy vehicles, felt, crayons, scissors, and glue. These are well marked and displayed, and they are within easy reach of the children. Children are expected to share all work and craft materials, which are kept in containers on shelves; scissors are not shared for reasons of safety, and a pair is provided for each child.

Mrs Clark has invested much effort and many personal resources in the classroom. In fact, she once told me that she did not like to be absent because of the valuable resources. Although this may be true, her conscientiousness and awareness of her responsibility to the children also seemed paramount. As I found out one day, this sense of duty also extended to the research project: 'Mrs Clark is sick, looks very pale ... came in because of the videotaping, says she didn't want to have to cancel it' (FN 5/12/97: 21).

Mrs Clark's class typically begins with roll call and a series of opening rituals and routines, centered on time and weather, numbers and letters, and rhymes and songs, leading to her presentation of the day's themes and activities. The children then engage in their first 'work' and/or craft activity, often related to literacy or numeracy. This is followed by snack and activity (or free play) time, during which the children are free to choose what they will do from a number of available options set up at various stations in the classroom (playhouse, sand table, computer, chalkboard, painting, puzzles, reading corner, listening center). After this, the children do another major activity, often of a craft-like nature, followed by story time, mail distribution, and closing exercises.

The work and craft activities are thematic, with everything tied into the learning objectives for the day or week. Some of the themes I observed focused on major holidays (e.g., Thanksgiving, Christmas, Chinese New Year) and topics such as dinosaurs, bees, and the wind. The children do the activities individually following group demonstration by the teacher.

The sequence of activities in Mrs Clark's classroom does not vary from day to day, except for an occasional 'upside-down day' when there is a visitor or unusual occurrence. The routine nature of the schedule allows the children to build up expectancies and make smooth transitions from one activity to the other. Mrs Clark cues them by switching lights off and on to signal any changes in activity. The children learn to respond to this cue very quickly. In my field notes for the second observation, I describe the smooth tempo that governs the class:

> I would describe the class as rhythmic, with not a pulse missed as the teacher moves the children from one routine or activity to the next. (FN 9/17/96: 1)

'This is the hardest part of the year – to get those rules established,' Mrs Clark commented to me in my first classroom observation (FN 9/13/96: 3). Indeed, I observed her often introducing and reviewing classroom rules that day and in the beginning weeks of the school year. In my first observation, for example, she carefully reviewed with the children the activity time rule of four children maximum in the house center, giving them reasons for the rule and vesting it (and at the same time herself) with authority by referring to it as 'Mrs Clark's Rule.' She involved the children and had them repeat the rule together as a community, coordinating it with body gestures, i.e., holding up their fingers and counting to four. She also encouraged the children as a community and individually to internalize rules, anticipate their actions in later situations, and help her reinforce rules to others.

Mrs Clark frequently encouraged children to appropriate her 'authoritative voice' by having them recall a rule themselves rather than by providing it directly herself. For example, when one girl asked if she could go to the puppets after finishing her snack, Mrs Clark prompted her with the question 'After snack time what do we do?' (FN 9/13/96: 3). She also reinforced proper observance of rules with words of approval and affective gestures, saying to a girl standing by a playhouse which already held the allowed maximum of four children, 'Did you count? That's a good girl,' patting her and directing her to a tub of animals to play with (FN 9/13/96: 4).

Mrs Clark assembled the children communally and carefully reviewed rules that were breached, giving reasons to show their non-arbitrary nature. She also justified her requests both routinely and in response to the rare hints of resistance, as in the following example:

> Allison has something in her hand. Mrs Clark: Allison, can you please put it back in the backpack please? Allison looks a little rebellious. Mrs Clark repeats: Sometimes toys in the circle cause disturbances. So it's better not to bring them to the circle. Allison goes and puts it away. (FN 9/24/96: 5)

Overall, Mrs Clark worked by suggestion rather than by direct reprimand or order, issuing positive statements as reminders and at the same time showing her approval of the behavior she valued (e.g., 'Most of my friends remembered to put scraps into the basket,' FN 9/24/96: 5). Although she was clearly in control, she did not appear authoritarian (Freire, 1985), and she was warm and respectful to the children. Without pausing for descriptive detail, I will simply note how freshly she seemed to approach each of the kindergarten sessions I observed and how engaged she was with the children. Even though she teaches two kindergarten sessions per day and has been teaching for many years, she seems to have escaped a commonly acknowledged danger of teaching, which is to fall into a routine. This, in my view, demonstrates a genuine respect and liking for the children and for her work.

Mrs Clark appears to have been successful in establishing habits and practices. At the end of the year, when I ask her if she would like to make any comments about the class as a whole, she describes her class as 'a dream year,' pointing to the children's happiness, their lack of arguing, their willingness to share with one another, and the little time she needs to spend in management and discipline:

Mrs Clark: This has been a dream year. This has been a most unusual year.... I wish I could duplicate it but *(sighs)* another year.
Elaine: What makes them (...) a dream?
Mrs Clark: Well, they're happy. There isn't a lot of bickering going on amongst them, arguing. They seem to share well. And I'm

not, I'm not spending time policing. I don't like being a policeman or nagging at them to clean up or nagging at them to do their best. (Teacher interview, 6/9/97)

As can be seen, Hari's teacher is pleased with her class and wishes she could duplicate it in the future.

Hari in School

The previous sections have introduced Hari and described some of the features of his community, school, teacher, and classroom as background for understanding the study. Now I turn to some descriptive details of Hari and his behavior and activities in school.

Hari attends school regularly and is always neatly and comfortably dressed, usually in a soft jersey shirt and denim pants. He wears a silver bracelet on his wrist, which is a Sikh religious practice. Hari is small and slight, but no less so than some of the other boys, two of whom are smaller than him. In the beginning months of school, he often brought Indian bread as one of his snacks but stopped doing this in November, when he started bringing an apple as his usual snack.

In my initial observations during the first few months, Hari struck me as quiet like many of the other English language learners, yet he did not appear particularly uneasy in the class. Hari generally participated in the classroom songs and opening routines, sometimes quietly, sometimes quite vigorously, and he occasionally contributed a brief answer to the teacher's questions. He sometimes interacted with the other children. During play time, I saw him most often with Kevin, an anglophone boy, or with Raj, a Punjabi-speaking girl. I also frequently saw him sitting beside either or both of these children in the circle where the children gathered for community activities or at the tables where they did their work and craft activities. As time went by, I also saw him with Manjit, the other Punjabi-speaking girl in his class.

On a few occasions in the first three months, I noticed that Hari worked at a slower pace than his table mates. In October, when the task was to draw three pumpkins in order of size, I observed Hari drawing one very small red pumpkin while his table mates were drawing three orange and black ones (FN 10/16/96: 4). In a December observation (12/10/96), Hari spent a long time making a Santa face and was the last child to finish, seeming more interested in merrily singing his version of a Santa verse circulating in the room and in contributing to the Christmas ambience than in the craft activity itself.

When Hari entered kindergarten, he used his home language, Punjabi, in the classroom as well as English. I now describe how he made use of this language and the changes I observed in his use of it during the year.

Use of Home Language

Because of the important relationship between language choice and identity, I took care to document Hari's use of his home language during the year of my observations. In the beginning months, I often observed Hari speaking Punjabi when interacting with Raj and Manjit, his Punjabi-speaking classmates, both at his own initiation and at theirs. In an early observation (9/17/96), for example, Hari initiates Punjabi and inter- acts actively with Raj, as they sit at the tables cutting out 'things that are red.' In another observation, the two children speak 'loudishly' in Punjabi when playing cars together at activity time (FN 9/30/96: 2).

Although Hari and his Punjabi-speaking classmates frequently speak their home language with one another, I also observed them code-switching to English. In September, Hari is sitting with Raj, Manjit, and an anglophone boy named Kevin, with whom he also affiliated in the beginning months of the year, and one other boy. The children are doing a craft activity. Hari code-switches from English to Punjabi and back to English according to his interlocutors. It is notable that he also does some self-talk in both Punjabi and English at this time.

> I hear Hari interacting in English with the other children: 'Where's mine.' 'I got a stem.' 'Yea.' Manjit and Raj talk in Punjabi in a short conversation initiated by Raj. Raj also addresses Hari in Punjabi.... I hear Hari in self-talk in Punjabi. Kevin (across from him) puts a piece of yellow construction paper on his head as if it is a hat, and Hari says to him 'I got brown,' referring to the color of his paper.... Hari says, 'You want glue?' looking up at Kevin as he continues to glue.... Raj and Manjit working quietly, Raj speaks to Manjit in Punjabi. She appears to be asking for glue and telling her to put it in middle of table. Hari speaks to Raj in Punjabi, then does some self-talk in English, picking up a brown crayon and saying, '... this brown.' Raj throws a few words of Punjabi into the air and picks up the glue. (FN 9/24/96: 1)

In one observation of the afternoon class in mid-January (1/16/97), Hari is at the round table coloring in a dinosaur during activity time; Ranjeet, one of Hari's frequent play partners, has gone to the carpeted area (i.e., circle) with a bucket of trucks and cars, and calls over to Hari in Punjabi. I am near Hari's table taking field notes. As I write in my field notes, Hari spontaneously addresses me. He tells me that Ranjeet is his friend and translates what Ranjeet says to him, thus acknowledging his identity as a Punjabi-speaker. He then gives me an unsolicited account of why he speaks English.

Hari:	(*to Elaine*) Ranjeet's my friend.
Elaine:	Who?
Hari:	Ranjeet is my friend.
...	
Ranjeet:	(*speaks Punjabi*).
Hari:	I tell, he said you wanna play that. I said I, I (working on).
Elaine:	(...)
Hari:	I no want, first I talking the Punjabi and now I, my mom and all the boys, big guys
Elaine:	Yea.
Hari:	Boys and over there.
Elaine:	Yea:
Hari:	It's (...) not to, it's not so::: (told) not in the house, it's just in the closed.
Elaine:	Oh.
Hari:	It's closed, we go in the (...) and he's tell me I English and now I talking the English.
Elaine:	Oh, you talk both, two, don't you. (Transcript, 1/16/97)

The field notes below illuminate this transcript:

> Hari tells me that Ranjeet is his friend; he explains what Ranjeet said when he spoke to him from the circle in Punjabi (i.e., he acts as interpreter). Then he tells me that he speaks Punjabi, that a boy took him in the corner and said speak English, so now I speak English (He tells me this in a matter of fact, seemingly accepting way).

> Ranjeet is speaking Punjabi. Baldev joins, speaks Punjabi. Hari speaks to Baldev in English: 'I wanna play that.' (FN 1/16/97: 7)

As can be seen, these field notes indicate that at this time Hari chooses to address his L1 peer, Baldev, in English, even though Baldev and Ranjeet are interacting in Punjabi.

In the first two months of the new year (January and February), I continued to see Hari with his Punjabi-speaking classmates, though less often than in the earlier months. Although he still sometimes spoke Punjabi with them, during January and February I observed no instance when he initiated the use of this language, as he had in the fall. Indeed, an incident in early February shows him initiating an interaction with the two girls in English and them deferring to his language choice.

> Manjit and Raj are at the table alone; Manjit tries to tell her how to fold her fan; they talk in Punjabi. Hari comes over, speaks to them in English. Raj and Manjit reply in English. (FN 2/6/97: 7)

One incident suggests that the children's common home language is a unifying force in threatening situations. When Raj is involved in a dispute with Claudia, a Polish-speaking classmate, Hari notices and walks over to defend Raj; Manjit does also; and the three children speak Punjabi (FN 2/10/97: 7).

A video excerpt in February (2/3/97) suggests that Hari may be investing in an identity as an English- rather than Punjabi-speaker at the tables. In this excerpt, the children are coloring and making groundhogs. Hari is seated across from Raj; Nadia, an Arabic-speaking girl, is seated at the head of the table to Hari's left.

Raj:	(*points to Hari's sheet, goes 'haw,' speaks in Punjabi*).
Hari:	(*looks at her*) Gray, making. (*Colors his groundhog, blending with brown that he has already colored. Says in English as he colors*). I wanna do it (buddy). That is good do that.
...	
Raj:	(*speaks in Punjabi to Hari, pointing to something behind her*).
	(*Hari looks at her, continues coloring his sheet, looks at Raj's sheet*).
Raj:	(*speaks in Punjabi to him*).
	(*Hari is coloring the whole time; he doesn't look at her*).
Hari:	(*taking scissors, begins to cut out his groundhog, gives quick glance toward Raj*) I want to cut this. I cutting at it now. (Video transcript, 2/3/97)

Hari ignores Raj much of the time and he uses English even though she repeatedly addresses him in Punjabi. At one later point, he initiates a conversational bid in English, first turning to Nadia and then turning and calling to Jason, who is one of the higher status males and is sitting with two other boys at the other end of the table:

Hari:	(*cutting out his groundhog, standing and turned toward Nadia*) I have movie (...) movie (*sits down, turns toward the other end of the table*).
Hari:	Jason, Jason, Jason. Jason, Jason.
Jason:	(Yea).
Hari:	I have (co) Power Ranger movie.

Jason:	Yea, I have that. Well, I have a Power Ranger movie too.
Hari:	I have too.
Jason or	
Kevin (?):	(So what) Power Rangers is for babies.
Hari:	I watch (…)
Raj:	Jason (*she speaks Punjabi*).
Hari:	Jason, you have most of the movies? (*Other children around Jason bid for his attention*).
Hari:	(*continues to cut, then looks up and calls out, showing his sheet mainly to Raj*) Look mine!
Raj:	(*laughs*).

As can be seen from the above transcript, Hari persists in addressing Jason but the conversation does not seem to go anywhere.

Hari associates much less with Raj and Manjit after the month of February, and his use of Punjabi in the morning class virtually disappears, while the two girls continue speaking Punjabi with one another. The following observation from my field notes in May shows him mocking the language:

> Hari comes into the reading center (Manjit is there). Raj is looking at a book of pictures of adult faces, looks like an alumni book or something (no words or few words in it). Hari is reading (or pretend reading) a book, sounds like he is reading Punjabi, exaggerating and mocking it. Raj (to me): He talk Punjabi. (FN 5/12/97: 21)

Hari also uses Punjabi in the afternoon session less and less frequently as the year goes by. In the first part of the school year, I observed Hari interacting frequently in both Punjabi and English with his two other Punjabi-speaking male peers in the afternoon (and also sometimes with Raj and Manjit there). However, though Hari continues to interact with all the Punjabi-speaking children through the rest of the year, he does so in English, and I observed him using Punjabi only once again in March, in an interchange in the blocks area towards the end of the day. In contrast, I observed the other Punjabi-speaking children in the afternoon class using Punjabi at least sometimes after that and even to the end of the year.

In the springtime interview, Mrs Clark relates to me that Hari polices the use of English in the afternoon class:

Mrs Clark:	And he will, he will tell the others. Ranjeet's notorious for speaking Punjabi. And he will tell him ah, 'Is English, you speak English, we're at English school' (*said with slight accent*). Makes my job easier when they, because I don't like to

say that to them, because it makes them maybe feel that their language is no good, but ah, I do like them to practice English at school. Hari kind of polices that.

Elaine: Are they speaking more English in the afternoon class?
Mrs Clark: I think so.
Elaine: Than they were at the beginning of the year?
…
Mrs Clark: I don't know if it's wishful thinking or if I'm too close to them, to the scene, but I think they are. (Teacher interview, 3/4/97)

As can be seen, Hari appropriates his teacher's 'authoritative voice' and enforces her wish for the children to practice English in the afternoon.

In the June interview, Mrs Clark confirms that Hari does not speak Punjabi in class. She mentions that when she asked him to speak to the newly arrived Punjabi-speaking boy, he declined to do so.

Elaine: How about his Punjabi, does he speak Punjabi?
Mrs Clark: I don't hear it.
Elaine: You don't hear it.
Mrs Clark: No, no. As a matter of fact, if I ask him to say something to Rajinder, he doesn't. I have to choose somebody else.
Elaine: Mmm, even though he spoke a lot at the beginning of the year, I recall.
Mrs Clark: He doesn't anymore. (Teacher interview, 6/9/97)

Mrs Clark recounts that when she asked one of the Punjabi-speaking children to explain something to the new boy in Punjabi, he did so whispering.

Mrs Clark: Ranjeet was so hesitant to do that, but he finally got up out of the chair and went around to where Rajinder was, and he whispered in his ear.
Elaine: Aha.
Mrs Clark: And told him. It's almost as if they are embarrassed to say anything in Punjabi in front of me. (Teacher interview, 6/9/97)

She laments this and openly speculates:

I'm sorry that I've made them feel that way. I certainly didn't do it intentionally. It's almost as if he thinks it is wrong to say, to speak Punjabi at school, which I guess maybe, I've encouraged English and he's self-conscious about it.

At another point in this interview, after she tells me that one particular

Punjabi-speaking boy speaks a lot of Punjabi in the afternoon class, and after I ask her about the others, she mentions that Hari speaks 'a little bit' of Punjabi but that this is inadvertent:

Elaine: Hari speaks Punjabi?
Mrs Clark: Yea, a little bit, not as much as the others. But he does occasionally. He'll find himself in the middle of a Punjabi conversation, you know, they're speaking around him, and I guess he just sort of falls into it.
Elaine: Falls into it.
Mrs Clark: Yea, I don't think he does it intentionally. (Teacher interview, 6/9/97)

In the home interview at the end of the school year, Hari's mother reports that he still speaks Punjabi with his grandmother, relatives, and others who speak only Punjabi and that he speaks English with friends. She thinks that he would prefer to speak English more so now than was the case before he started kindergarten, mentioning that he used to speak Punjabi with his Punjabi-speaking classmates but now prefers to speak English. Hari confirms this in the home interview; when asked which language he prefers, he says, 'I like to speak English.'

Hari's mother also says that he is less interested in Punjabi movies and music than he was before starting kindergarten. At home he likes watching children's videos in English, and he asks his grandfather to take them out of the public library for him. He also watches TV in English, claiming first choice in the family when his favorite shows are on. Despite these preferences, his mother feels that he still speaks and understands Punjabi well, mentioning that he can retell the oral stories that his grandmother tells him in Punjabi.[3] The home interviewer confirms this, judging that he can speak Punjabi fluently.

Hari's Use of English

Hari seemed to have difficulty pronouncing English; in particular, he had a retroflex 'r.' The teacher and other children seemed to be able to understand him, while I sometimes found this difficult. I frequently observed Hari in self-talk in both Punjabi and English in the first few months, but during the course of the year he apparently gave this up.

When using English, Hari in the beginning months spoke mainly with a few words, elliptical phrases, or short sentences. He made his meaning known, enabled by his use of gesture, repetition and rephrasing and by the collaboration of his interlocutors. In November, he cedes his place at the computer, pointing to those who can go next and saying, 'He, after finished; then you, then me' (FN, 11/4/96: 4). On the same day, when drawing at the tables, he effectively counters his classmate Kevin's claim to having a superior drawing by taking his words and suiting them to his own ends:

Kevin: Mine looks better than yours.

Hari: Mine is your better (*not very clearly enunciated*). (Video transcript, 11/4/96)

At another time, Hari runs up to me at the end of the morning and tells me that he is going home, repeating and rephrasing, so that I at least partially understand what he means: 'I going home. (Elaine: Why?) Because I going, my dad and mom, going home. No, he going a plane' (FN 11/18/96: 10). As I later learn by asking Mrs Clark, Hari is going home to accompany his parents to the airport.

Hari increased his participation in the classroom community over the year. As he did, he used language for a greater range of functions than he did initially; he also spoke in longer and syntactically more complex sentences. By early March, I had documented examples of temporal, causal and hypothetical clauses. In early February (2/6/97), in sharing he calls out after a classmate has talked about her ice skates: 'I have ice skates and when I was four, I fall down' (FN 2/6/97: 2). In early March, he volunteers a reply to a Block Parent's question: 'If you get hurt and we can go home, tell our parent our friend is hurt and call to hospital' (FN 3/4/97: 8).

By spring, Hari also uses a greater range of verb forms than in the beginning months; from January onwards I noted him using the past tense, in addition to present tense and present progressive aspect (as determined by context). In mid-spring, I noted that he began to use the past progressive aspect also: 'You're were just looking' (Transcript, 3/12/97); 'Last night when I was watching TV with my dog ...' (FN 4/23/97: 2). As well, in mid-spring, I observed him using the full auxiliary in the present progressive (e.g., 'the boy is walking on the road,' Transcript, 3/4/97), whereas previously he had used no auxiliary or the elided form (e.g., 'Kevin eating,' Transcript, 2/25/97; 'he's not going,' Video transcript, 2/3/97).

Viewed from a traditional second language perspective, Hari made many 'errors' in his verb forms; like other second language learners, he showed great variability in the coexistence of correct and incorrect forms, both within the same stretch of speech and across time. In the following example, Hari expresses the past tense of the verb 'to eat' in three ways:

Mrs Clark: Oh, and what was it?

Hari:	(*doesn't reply*).
Mrs Clark:	M and M's?
Hari:	(*nods his head*).
Mrs Clark:	M and M's starts with M? Did you eat them all?
Hari:	No, I ated, I ate them a long time ago, I eated all.
Mrs Clark:	Did you? (Video transcript, 3/3/97)

As can be seen, Hari first overgeneralizes the -ed past ending ('I ated') and self-corrects to the standard form ('I ate'). He then overgeneralizes again, but this time using the present stem of the verb ('I eated all'), thereby echoing the teacher's question, 'Did you eat them all?'

Hari also shows variability in tense selection, sometimes switching from present to past and back to present or vice versa. This occurs mainly in his circle narrations, usually not in his responses to question/answer exchanges. For example, when the teacher asks the classroom for someone to tell her the steps in the germination of a frog, Hari consistently uses the past tense to answer:

Hari:	(*breaking in right away*) First the egg, then he cracked and then he (*children whispering 'tadpole'*) and then he growed bigger, the tail was short, then he turned to a frog.
Some children:	[frog

(Transcript, 5/26/97)

When he narrates his own experiences or recounts a story, his tense usage is more variable. In the following example, Hari recounts a Charlie Brown video on kite-flying after Claudia tells about her kite-flying experience:

Claudia:	You know, when I was at the beach, my brother went to buy me a kite and, and then we went back to the spot that we were and I was flying the kite.
…	
Hari:	Uh, uh, I see Charlie Brown, he's flying the kite, well he's come down and down and down.
Mrs Clark:	Did it crashed on him?
Hari:	Yah, yah and he the kite get all around him, and his head and he, he, get off of his head and and it just like that rope (*pointing to the string in the picture with the poem on it*).
Mrs Clark:	Oh, the string, hmm, hmm.
Hari:	Yah and, and his hands got all and he, he goes to the dog teacher, and he, and he said, and he, and her, the teacher, dog teacher said um 'why you got that kite on there?' (Video transcript, 3/3/97)

Although Claudia and the teacher use the past tense, Hari tells his story in the present, perhaps to maintain his presence in the story and express its immediacy. In his final statement, he switches to the past perhaps to distance himself from this immediacy and report indirect dialogue.

Discussion

Consistent with Heller's (1987) emphasis on the importance of language in gaining access to social relationships, sharing a common first language with some of the other children seems to have provided Hari with a ready source of affiliation as he maneuvered the new environment of the classroom in the early months. In the beginning months, Hari uses his home language freely with his Punjabi-speaking classmates. Fairly early on, he code-switches between English and Punjabi. The early example from my field notes shows how Hari is able to code-switch between his two languages according to his interlocutors, showing the complex bilingual skills noted by many researchers (e.g., Milroy & Muysken, 1995; Orellana, 1994; Vasquez *et al.*, 1994).

As the year goes by, Hari ceases to use Punjabi and his two Punjabi-speaking classmates defer to his language preference, addressing him in English, even though they speak to each other in Punjabi. However, he still uses Punjabi with them in solidarity. Hari and Manjit's defense of Raj in her dispute with the Polish child and their subsequent tripartite conversation in Punjabi resonate with Dabène and Moore's (1995) argument that language should be seen as much more than a simple means of communication and can be invested with symbolic boundary functions (p. 24).

Hari shows a clear preference for English earlier than the other Punjabi-speaking children. On one occasion, he ignores Raj much of the time, uses English even though she repeatedly addresses him in Punjabi, and initiates a conversational opener to one of the anglophone males in English, suggesting an identity choice as an English-speaker. Many researchers (Bourne, 1988; Leung *et al.*, 1997; Norton Peirce, 1995; Schecter & Bayley, 1997; Siegal, 1996) argue that language choice involves 'acts of identity,' a term derived from LePage and Tabouret-Keller (1985) to symbolize the kind of identity the speaker wants to communicate in an interaction.

Many observers (Dabène, 1994; Deprez, 1994; Pease-Alvarez & Winsler, 1994; Wong Fillmore, 1989) have noted that minority language children shift their language of preference to the dominant language when they go to school, and Hari and most of his Punjabi-speaking peers seem to be no exception to this. However, Hari seems to show the shift sooner, both in comparison to his female peers in the morning session, who begin to speak English rather than Punjabi to one another in April, and in comparison to all the Punjabi-speaking children in the afternoon session.

Hari does not usually address me extensively when I observe him.[4] It is interesting to speculate on why he chooses to do so when he tells me why he no longer uses Punjabi in school and uses English to break into Baldev's and Ranjeet's Punjabi conversation. It is possible that my presence as an observer in this situation may have prompted Hari to represent himself and articulate his identity to me. Consistent with the view of identity in the present work, Hodges (1998) urges us to consider that 'we are not born with complex identities but rather that we *become* 'multiplied' through ongoing sociality' (pp. 272–273). The incident suggests how this multiplication might have occurred, both through the personal experience Hari recounts and through my presence as an observer, which may have prompted him to represent himself and thus bring this multiplication to further awareness.

Deprez (1994) argues that bilingual children are conscious of using two different languages at an early age, as shown by the way they adjust speech to their interlocutor (s) and their self-correction and experimentation with new words. Hari's later attempts to encourage the other children to speak English show another aspect of this consciousness, relating to his perception of the relative status of his two languages. As the teacher discourse data show, Hari received implicit messages concerning which language was of most worth.

Although Hari prefers English in school, he has not abandoned Punjabi, continues to use it at home, and speaks it with his grandmother when she is in the school. This is consistent with research showing that there can be considerable variation in home language use and maintenance (Deprez, 1994; Pease-Alvarez & Winsler, 1994). It also illustrates the importance of grandparents and other factors, such as travel to the home country, in providing functional opportunities for using and maintaining the home language (Dagenais & Day, 1998; Deprez, 1994; Schecter & Bayley, 1997).

In his first year of kindergarten, Hari also had many functional opportunities for using English; at the end of the chapter, I briefly described how his language grew over the year, focusing mainly on his verb usage and noting the considerable variability I observed. Although variability is a controversial issue for SLA researchers (Ellis, 1994), it is consistent with the view of language as dynamic and situated speech activity.

Bakhtin emphasized that speaking is not an individual act and that when we speak, we ventriloquate and transform what we have heard from others. We fashion our utterances both according to the voices we have heard and those to whom we are speaking. The example of Hari's verb corrections in his dialogue with Mrs Clark shows that while he has an underlying rule for forming the past tense in English and 'knows' that there are exceptions, Hari is aware of the social and political conditions under which he speaks and fashions his response accordingly. Bakhtin's insistence that some interactions have more sociohistorical authority invested in them than others and his concept of language as a personal resource for claiming a voice seem to me appropriate for understanding Hari's tense usage in the other two examples I provided.

Summary

In the first part of this chapter, I provided contextual and background information on Hari, his school, teacher, and classroom. I then examined the affiliations he made with children of his home language, focusing on questions of language choice and identity. I presented data showing Hari's complex bilingual skills and some of the identity choices he seemed to be making as an English-speaker. I showed how he ceased using Punjabi in the classroom and distanced himself from his Punjabi-speaking identity, providing data from the teacher's discourse to show how implicit messages concerning the relative value of his two languages might have been conveyed to him. Finally, I provided some descriptive detail on Hari's linguistic development in his second language, noting how he used English resourcefully and in consideration of his addressee. Hari's kindergarten year illustrates the sociocultural perspective that language learning, language choice, social interaction, and identity are inextricably interwoven.

Notes
1. When we conducted the study, a new school was being planned; it was built and ready for occupancy in the 1998–1999 school year.
2. In this transcript and all those that follow, items enclosed within single parentheses and not italicized indicate transcriptionist doubt; items enclosed within single parentheses and italicized indicate pauses and details of the conversational scenes or various characterizations of the talk. For further details on transcription conventions, see the Appendix.
3. In an informal conversation held between Hari's grandmother and Kunwal, the Punjabi-speaking researcher, at the end of the interview, Hari's grandmother relates that he speaks Punjabi with her and also mentions that he can retell the Punjabi stories she tells him, both in Punjabi and in English.
4. With respect to Hari's interactions with me, his interactions up to this time comprise occasionally showing me his work and talking to me at the change of an activity; e.g., when it is time for recess, he leaves saying, 'I playing' (10/28/96); when he has to go home instead of staying for lunch and for the afternoon session, he says to me, 'I going home ...' (11/18/96).

Chapter 5
Hari and his Classmates

> Language is not only an instrument of communication or even of knowledge, but also an instrument of power. A person speaks not only to be understood but also to be believed, obeyed, respected, distinguished.... Competence implies the power to impose reception.
>
> (Bourdieu, 1977: 648)

In this chapter, I focus on the social and political dimensions of Hari's peer relationships, and I examine his interactions with some of the classmates with whom I saw him most frequently during the year. My investigation centers on the following question derived from my understanding of Lave and Wenger's (1991) work:

> What are the social and political dimensions of Hari's relationships with some of his classmates and how do these affect possibilities for learning?

In the first section, I focus on Hari's relationship with Kevin, one of the children with whom Hari affiliated in the beginning months of the school year, showing the possibilities and constraints in this relationship. In the second section, I trace Hari's participation with the larger subgroup of children of which the two boys were a part. I also examine the identities he displays in different social networks and in different oral practices. In the last section, I examine power relations and positioning practices to show the kinds of identities on offer to Hari and to help understand the kinds of participation I observed. Throughout, I also discuss strategies Hari uses in responding to the positions assigned and in negotiating a more powerful identity.

Social Relations

Hari and Kevin, an English-speaking boy classmate, affiliated with one another in the beginning months of the year. I frequently saw them together at activity time, seated by one another in the circle, and together at the tables for snack time and work activities. An early observation in September shows them 'sitting very close' and sharing resources, as they color and cut an apple out of construction paper:

Hari goes and gets a pair of scissors; Kevin puts out his hand and says, 'I need it.' Hari: 'Share, share' (gives it to Kevin and gives a toothy smile). (FN 9/24/96: 5)

Many of my observations suggest that Kevin was helpful to Hari in the early months. The following examples show some ways in which he helps to hold Hari's place at the tables, both linguistically and socially.

In October (10/21/96) as Hari and Kevin sit by one another eating their snacks at snack time, the following conversation was recorded at their table:

Hari: Flower (eat it)
Hari: Flower
Kevin: (*to Thomas*) Yew, yew, his his his his his baby, he ate a flower, not Hari, his ah baby brother I think or something ate a flower. (Transcript, 10/21/96)

Kevin repeats and retells something Hari has told him to Thomas, a child at the table. Thomas and another child, Sue, subsequently join in and continue the topic of family members and eating. Hari's more expert peer thus helps him to have a place in the communicative chain at the table.

In another snack time in October (10/16/96), one of the other boys, Allan, asserts that Hari is not strong, and Kevin counters by ventriloquating the teacher, who at every snack time circulates around the room and says 'healthy' or 'not healthy' as she points to the individual children's snacks.

Hari is saying something like 'I er I got one' about the top of his container. The children at the table are talking. I hear Allan say (about Hari) 'He's not strong.' A few seconds later, Kevin, referring to Hari (who has eaten an apple for snack time), says 'Apples are healthy; they make muscles.' (FN 10/16/96: 9)

By linking to the practice of a more powerful member of the community (i.e., the teacher) and elaborating on it ('He eats healthy stuff. Apples are healthy; they make muscles'), Kevin supports Hari and legitimizes his place in the face of Allan's claim.

During the same snack time, Hari also has the opportunity to observe Kevin and Allan engaging in a playful language practice involving repetition:

Kevin says, referring to snack tub (he had eaten most of the popcorn in it): 'Allan, guess what, I put gas in here.' Hari looks up at me and smiles

(I think he has understood that Kevin is joking). Kevin says: 'Allan, I put Slurpy in here.' Hari listens to Allan and Kevin interchange about this.... Hari points to his apple and says something like 'I ... gas in here.' (He has pronunciation difficulties; 'here' sounds like 'her'). (FN 10/16/96: 8)

Hari indicates by the way he looks up at me and smiles that he understands the 'key' (Hymes, 1974) for the interaction, which in this case is playful. After observing further, he hooks into and participates in the language practice of his table mates and affiliates with them. Hari's attempt at participation is received in this particular example, but this is not always the case, as we will later see.

Kevin and Hari enjoy amicable relations over the early months of the school year and are often seen together both at the tables and at activity time. Indeed, in December, I noted that the two boys join one another for the same craft activity and for snacks on an occasion when their class spends the morning in the school's other kindergarten classroom (FN 12/9/96). However, there are also occasions of tension in their relationship. On one occasion, Kevin rebuffs Hari when he comes to sit by him at the table. Hari then goes and sits at the other end of the table. Kevin sits with another classmate, explicitly refusing to identify with Hari.

Allan: If I were you, I'll sit next to Hari.
Kevin: If I were you, I would too.
Kevin: I don't want to be like him.
Allan: Me too. (FN 10/21/96: 4)

Kevin and Allan form a link through the repetition and interanimation of voices in the two couplets, and at the same time they reinforce Hari's position as not wanted.

Later during activity time when Hari and Kevin are playing cars together, Kevin tries to exert his power when Hari does not comply with him (Kevin: 'I'm the real boss here. I don't want you to play,' FN 10/21/96: 5). Kevin does not share resources and repeatedly tries to direct the play, correcting Hari as he moves his truck all over the mat ('No big giant truck on the road. No trucks allowed') or as he uses his car like an airplane ('No, your car can't fly. It needs doors like these'). And when Hari slams his jeep hard onto the road, Kevin chides, 'Hari, you're not being very good' (Transcript, 10/21/96). Kevin again tries to control the play ('Like this, that's why they can jump'), and Hari resists by folding his arms and/or saying 'I don't want to play' (FN 10/21/96: 6). This pattern of domination and resistance continues, as the following excerpt from the transcript shows:

Kevin: ... Hari, fine, don't play then, don't play.
Hari: if (...) [car
                 (*Hari folds his arms again*).
Kevin: (*annoyedly*):[No::: you can't put it here (...) you you already
                 had a jump (...) right, this guy and this guy....
Hari: ... (play)
(...)
                 (*Hari is still mad; Kevin goes right up to Hari*).
Kevin: Hari, you, okay fine, your cars can jump. Hari, I said your
                 cars could jump. (...) Hari, Hari, your cars can jump.
...
                 (*Hari refuses to talk to him*).
Kevin: Hari, fine, Hari, oh then go away (...)
                 (*Hari gets up and leaves. He goes to the block center*).
Kevin: Hey, Hari (...)
...
                 Hari, Hari, Hari, you can play.
Hari: I not playing that. (Transcript, 10/21/96)

Kevin annoyedly dismisses Hari and again tries to control the play. When Hari resists by folding his arms and refusing to play, Kevin goes right up to him; as he is taller than Hari, he may be trying to exert a certain control with his body. He tries to accommodate Hari by letting his cars jump, but Hari refuses to talk to him. Kevin then dismisses him: 'Hari, fine, Hari, oh then go away.' Hari goes to the block area and Kevin follows him, telling him that he can play. Hari again refuses him. It is the end of activity time, and the two boys return to the carpet to clean up the cars. As this example shows, Hari has some simple but effective strategies for tenaciously resisting the position Kevin offers him; the following example shows other strategies he employs.

In late January, there are some troubling signs in the relationship between Hari and Kevin, signaled by a teasing incident observed at the beginning of snack time. Kevin and Jason are chatting to one another as they eat their snacks at the long table, where Hari is also sitting eating an apple. Hari breaks in:

Hari: Kevin, don't you know?
Jason: Mine was stick the, stick stick Superman's, on my birthday it
                 was stick, stu, stick, stu, Superman's heart back into place.

Hari:	(*singingly*) Spiderman, Spiderman, what the (…) what the (…) Spiderma:::n (*ends in rising intonation*). You know Spiderman?
Kevin:	(*holding out a slice of pear*) Hari, Hari, eat some pear. I just joking you know. Hari doesn't like pear (*teasing voice*), mmm mmmm (*teasingly*).
Jason:	Hari sometimes is a copycatter.
Hari:	What?
Kevin:	Nothing. Nothing. We were just um say[ing
Hari:	[I
Kevin:	[How nice you are.
Hari:	No:, I know is what you say, I no wanna tell you.
Jason:	I know. What do we say?
Hari:	I no wanna tell you (*rising intonation*).
Kevin:	Okay, I'll t, (*lowers voice*) tell you, sometimes you're such a copycatter.
Hari:	What?
Kevin:	(*whispers to Jason*) Hari (…)
Hari:	Copycat?
Jason:	Sometimes you're such a copycatter.
Kevin:	Well I didn't say that, I didn't say it, I didn't say it. Jason did, he said it in <u>my</u> ear. Don't blame me, blame <u>him</u>.
Jason:	Yeah, blame Kevin. Don't blame me, blame Kevin. (Transcript, 1/23/97)

Initially, Hari bids for Kevin's attention by using the conversational opener 'Don't you know,' which he had begun to use frequently around this time. He attempts a second bid by playfully singing and repeating something about Spiderman. Perhaps he is also echoing Jason's talk to Kevin about sticking Superman's heart into place. Kevin holds out a slice of pear and starts to tease Hari. Jason subordinates Hari by telling him that he is a copycatter. Hari asks, 'What?'; Kevin does not tell him and then retracts the insult. (In this classroom, one of the main uses of the term 'copycatter' or 'copycat' was to subordinate and/or exclude a child.)

As in the earlier incident in the fall when he resisted Kevin's domination ('I don't want to play'), Hari tries to set up a counter-discourse, centered on his knowledge of, but refusal to repeat, the insult: 'I know is what you say, I no wanna tell you.' His playful tone at this point suggests that he tries to join in with the two boys. He changes position several times during this incident, betraying his unease ('Hari under table, then standing by coat rack eating apple, then back to table,' FN 1/23/97: 30).

Hari is not successful in his counter-discourse, for the boys have other linguistic resources. Later, at the table, I recorded the following interchange:

Kevin: (*to Jason*) He's really weird …
Jason: (*about their work*) I don't really like this you know that much.
Hari: I'n I'n the weird. (Transcript, 1/23/97)

Kevin makes the statement to Jason about Hari, 'He's really weird,' as if after having helped construct Hari as 'weird,' he declares him to be so. And Hari repeats this to the boys: 'I'n I'n the weird.' Perhaps, as an English language learner, Hari does not know what the adjective 'weird' means and therefore repeats and accepts it. Perhaps he intends a kind of playful counter-tease by this repetition. Whatever the reasons, Kevin's assertion positions Hari outside the bounds of normality.

At the conclusion of this interaction (and here I summarize from my field notes), Hari puts a battery on the table (this seems almost like a challenge to Jason), Jason grabs it, Hari asks for it back and the two boys jostle playfully; Hari finally gets the battery back (FN 1/23/97). Thus, realizing perhaps that he cannot win through language, Hari initiates a counter-challenge with a material resource to defuse the situation. This diverts the teasing from the linguistic arena and allows Hari to regain some control.

My observations after this incident suggest that Hari's relationship with Kevin seems to weaken over the remaining part of the year. For example, I did not observe the two boys with one another at activity time, except for a few occasions at the computer and on one occasion when they play separately on car mats. Hari begins to play mainly by himself during activity time and, as time goes by, with Casey, a newcomer to the class in late January. This contrasts with the first part of the year, when, during activity time, I often observed him socializing with Kevin, his two Punjabi-speaking girl classmates, and, more rarely, with some of the other boys, in particular Sean.

Participation

Hari does, however, continue to maintain his affiliation with the larger subgroup of boys which includes Kevin and Jason. He sits among the boys in circle activities and at the tables where they tend to gather for craft, work activities and snacks, sometimes sitting by Kevin or Jason or even between them in these settings.

As the year goes by, I noticed Hari growing increasingly industrious in the craft and work activities at the tables, seeming to prefer to listen to those chatting around him rather than to participate in their conversation. In the following example from May, the children are making a pig; as they do, Casey, Kevin, Jason, and Allan chat with one another about various topics, including their baseball teams. Hari works quietly and industriously, yet is aware of what is going on, handing Kevin a pink crayon when he calls out for one.

> Hari working, doesn't seem to be paying attention to what they are saying.... When Kevin calls out, 'Hey, where's the pink that I was using?' Hari immediately finds it for him.... Hari picks out crayons he is going to use from the boxes on the table, saying as he does, 'red ... red, pink, any pink?' ... Casey and Kevin are interchanging about baseball teams.... Hari is quiet and busy through all this. (FN 5/6/97: 7)

Hari is not always as quiet as in the preceding example. When he participates verbally at the tables, his talk mainly concerns remarking on the materials or task (as in the field note excerpt above), calling attention to his work ('Look, a bunny rabbit. I a bunny rabbit,' Transcript, 3/26/97), and as we shall see later, making interjections in some of the verbal play. However, he rarely participates in the conversational talk at the tables. More significantly, he does not show increasing participation in this kind of talk, as one might expect from the growing fluency which he shows in using English in other settings, for example, in the circle activities (see Chapter 7). This is particularly marked in the case of narration.

Although he often narrates personal experiences in sharing and at other times in the circle during the year (where a powerful ally, his teacher, holds his place for him; see Chapter 7), I did not observe Hari introduce little anecdotes about himself at the tables, either in dyadic or in multi-party interactions, as did the other children:

Jason:	(*singing a little bit*) Power (...) power
Kevin:	One time it was really windy and the power (...) went out and I had to sleep with my mummy.
Jason:	Scaredy cat!
Kevin:	Oh yea, I (will I will) like my mummy.
Jason:	So (...) scaredy cat (...)
Child:	(...) (pretend) you're camping in the woods without your mom. (Transcript, 10/28/96)

Perhaps Hari finds the possibility of challenge or teasing, as in this particular interaction, too threatening. Yet, I note that he did not seem particularly hesitant to expose himself in some of the ritual boasting or by calling attention to his work. Hari does not seem to talk about personal matters, at least amongst his peers at the tables; it seems that the assistance Kevin provided in hooking Hari into the multi-party talk in the fall, that seemed so promising then, did not become fruitful (see earlier example, Transcript 10/21/96: '... his ah baby brother I think or something ate a flower').

Perhaps it is more difficult for English language learners to break into or initiate multi-party interactions at the table than it is in circle time. Yet, I observed some occasions in which the other English language learners in Hari's class join in the narrative talk at the tables. The following brief excerpt comes from a longer interaction, in which Raj, Hari's Punjabi-speaking peer, joins in with two other classmates who had been telling each other about their dreams about dinosaurs. Raj first inserts herself into the chain by repeating her two classmates, and later briefly recounts her own dream, which is met with acceptance.

Raj: I have the dinosaurs coming at me too, know what, long (head) one.
Allison: What dream did you have?
Raj: Um, tyrannosaurus rex. (Transcript, 4/15/97)

In addition, I observed occasions when the English language learners engaged in lengthy storytelling; I also observed growth in this area during the year. For example, Manjit tells Raj a long story about herself in May (Transcript, 5/20/97). Such examples do not appear in my data for Hari, however.[1]

Overall, Hari keeps a low profile at the tables, seeming to participate in some kinds of talk but not claiming spaces in the narratives. Later, I will discuss some of the positioning practices that show the kinds of identities some of his classmates offer to Hari and what these identities suggest for the stance he takes up and the kinds of identities he actually displays. Here, I focus on showing how Hari takes on different identities in different social networks and in different oral practices.

The clearest examples of Hari adopting a different identity involve song, rhyme, and story-reading, in which the children engage either alone or in small spontaneous groupings. On these occasions, and in conjunction mainly with some of the other English language learners, Hari takes on a more powerful identity and challenges his peers. These examples provide a striking contrast to the more reticent identity he usually displays with the boys in his class.

At dismissal time, as the children prepare to leave, I record the following interchange between Hari and Claudia, who are in the area near the table where I am seated with the tape recorder.

Claudia:	(…) have a big HEART.
Hari:	Dicky dicky dinosaur eating the plant.
Claudia:	Ha, ha, ha. Dicky dicky dinosaur eating some hearts.
Hari:	Dicky dicky dinosaur eating some plant, jump in the (rock) and drink the water.
Claudia:	Dicky dicky dinosaur comes to our lake.
Hari:	[Dicky dicky
Claudia:	[Dicky dicky dinosaur eat some plant [dicky dicky
Hari:	[dicky, dicky dinosaur swimming on the water. (Transcript, 1/23/97)

This interchange takes place three to five minutes after the teacher had read the children a rhyming story 'Dicky, dicky dinosaur.' In the interchange, Claudia provides an opener; Hari challenges her; Claudia, laughing, then repeats her initial opener. Hari counters with a list-like challenge, to which Claudia responds. The two children start speaking together and vie for control of the conversation. Hari wins out, speaking over Claudia and seizing control.

Another example of Hari displaying a more powerful identity occurs in late March (3/26/97) at snack time, when the children are free to engage in a brief activity after they finish eating. Hari goes to the carpeted area where Raj and Manjit are standing talking, and he picks out a rather large book, saying loudly, 'I want to read this book' (Transcript, 3/26/97). The book contains colorful illustrations of crayons. Raj, Manjit, and Eva join him as he sits down with the book and starts turning the pages, pretending to read.

Hari:	Crayon is (*leading intonation and pause*)
Raj:	White
Manjit:	No, purple, red.
Hari:	No. Crayon is different color and you can (…)
…	
Hari:	(*singingly*) And color is everywhere! Color is every[where!
Raj:	[RED, purple, RED, purple, RED, [purple.
Manjit:	[No, purple.
Hari:	And color, you can every (*pause*) you can color everywhere in the paper.
…	

(Transcript, 3/26/97)

Hari is clearly in control; however, through leading intonation and pause, he gives the other children space to contribute. He creates and elaborates his own text and refrain: 'Color is everywhere.' He then initiates a repetitive 'I like' sequence, in which the other children engage.[2] But it is he who finalizes the conversation.

The composition of the group changes and now includes Hari, Raj, Sean, and later Paula. Hari continues to turn the pages:

Hari: Crayon is everywhere!
Child: (...)
Hari: Crayon can color

...

Raj: (*singingly*) I like (red).
Hari: (*pointing to crayon illustrations in book*) I like, I, I=
Raj: =I like
Hari: (*banging with every 'this'*) I like this this this this this this this this this [this this
Raj: [I like this this this this this this this
Hari: Color is everywhere!
Raj: I like this too.
Hari: Color is. We can color. We (*pause*) can (*pause*) color.
                (*The page in the book shows a few children sitting around some large crayons*). (Transcript, 3/26/97)

Hari pretend reads, 'Crayon is everywhere!', 'Crayon can color.' Raj breaks in and Hari engages with Raj in 'I like' play, enthusiastically banging with his fingers as he points to the crayon illustrations in the book. Hari repeats the refrain, 'Color is everywhere!', and again pretend reads, using the inclusive 'we' as they look at a page showing children sitting around some large crayons: '... We (*pause*) can (*pause*) color.'

The subsequent transcript and my field notes indicate that Hari invites Paula and another girl (Nadia), who later joins the circle, to look at the book, while he retains control of it. He also playfully interchanges with Raj, using a highly valued literacy practice, syllable segmentation, in the process:

Raj: Crayons in the house. Crayons in the house.
Hari: Crayon. Cray on the, cray on the. (Transcript, 3/26/97)

He then stands up and waves his hands over his head, saying happily, 'Crayon is everywhere!'

In this incident, Hari positions himself powerfully as the creator and elicitor of text. He provides openings and creates occasions in which all children can join in when he picks up the crayon book and orchestrates (he initially uses a leading intonation, providing a pause in which the other children can answer), maintaining his position throughout. He offers the book to others, but he also actually remains in control of it the whole time. Interestingly, all the children involved are other English language learners in the class, except for Sean, an anglophone boy, whom I rarely observed to be other than a quiet bystander in classroom activities. The communal situation of singing, practiced mainly by the girls in the class, perhaps provides Hari with a passageway where he can position himself powerfully and at the same time create community.

Politics and Positioning

The preceding examples show that Hari reveals a different identity when participating in different social networks and when involved in different oral practices. Sometimes, and particularly in conjunction mainly with other English language learners (who are all girls), Hari is able to lead and to have his contributions repeated. He assumes a powerful identity in these situations and learns that he can be at the same time challenging and communal. When he is at the tables with other children, for example, the anglophone boys, he seems to be positioned as not worthy of attention; his innovations are not taken up, or if they are, they are preempted.

This is particularly clear in the case of the language games in which the children sometimes engage when they work together. Hari contributes to the games initiated by the other children, but his contributions are not productive; the others do not take them up and continue them:

Allan:	Who's ever been in America, put up their ha::nds.
Sue:	What
Jason:	This [isn't
Sue:	[I went to Jamaica.
Jason:	This isn't America.
Sue:	This is, I may, I go to [Jamaica.
Jason:	[This is the States.
Sue:	I [go to Jamaica.
Jason:	[This is the United States.
Sue:	I go to Jamaica.
Sue:	Whoever go to Jamaica, put up their ha::nds.
	(*Jason and Hari put up their hands*).
Child:	Last
Sue:	(*pointing to those with hands up*) You did, you did, you did.
Sue:	Whoever go to the 'nited States, put up their hand.
Sue:	Da da da da da da, 1, 2, 3, 4, 5, 6

(Sue or another child going: 1, 2, 3, 4, okay, 5. Children laughing).

Allan: (*looks around table and says to Sue*) (Boys, there are lots of) boys on this table.

Sue: (*smiles*) Yea and one girl, that's me.

Hari: Who want t, who [went in the

Allan: [Who's the slowest, put up their hands.
(All children put up their hands).

**Sue
or Allan:** (*pointing to others*) Okay, you're the slowest, you're the slowest, okay (*laughing*).

Hari: Who go in, whose who whose mom and dad go to 'me:rica, stand up. My dad is, my mom and dad go to 'merica.

Sue: I go to Jamaica.

Child: I go

Child: It was so hot there.

Child: I know … oh I go to die there.

Sue: They don't have phones.

Child: What?

Sue: They don't have phones there.

Child: I know that.

Sue: And you know what there

Jason: When I got there, when I got there, my dad was at a telephone, I'm like I'm gonna go up and call my dad and my mom's like there's no phones here.

Hari: Look mine … (Transcript, 5/12/97)

In this example from mid-May, Allan initiates a round of a game commonly heard at the tables; this revolves around the frame: 'Whoever …, put up their hands.' Allan's initiative uses the US as an example. Sue tries to gain a hold by claiming that she has gone to Jamaica and she resists Jason's repeated corrections that Jamaica is not in the States. She successfully takes over the game, again resisting when Allan tries to exclude or subordinate her by making a gender-referenced statement that there are all boys at the table.

When Hari initiates a contribution, Allan seizes on the time it takes him to phrase it. He interrupts with a comment referring to Hari's slowness: 'Who's the slowest put up their hands.' Hari resists Allan's attempt to thwart him and persists in his contribution, taking care to justify its truth value ('my mom and dad go to 'merica') and inventing a variation ('stand up' vs. 'put up hands'), which may allow him to seize a place without conflicting with the position the others have had. He is not successful, however. Although his contribution is in fact quite resourceful and provides a way of extending the game beyond its limits, the others ignore it. Sue intervenes and gains the others' attention in an interchange involving Allan, Jason, and herself. Finally, Hari bids for attention again, showing his work and saying, 'Look mine.'

On this and other occasions, Hari was positioned as lower in status; his participation at the tables seemed thereby constrained. Some of the data show that elements of the discourse in the fall in which Hari was positioned as not strong and not wanted (10/16/96, 'He's not strong') occur again in the spring. For example, in May (5/6/97), at the end of activity time, when Hari picks up the bucket of cars to put it away, his classmate Allan charges, 'You're not that strong' (FN 5/6/97: 12).

Also in May (5/26/97), Kevin asserts his (and the other children's) superior physical prowess over Hari, teaming up with Jason as was the case with the teasing incident in January. The children are seated at the long table doing a work activity. Jason and Kevin challenge one another (Kevin: 'I'm taller'; Jason: 'I can go faster'). Hari is working and Kevin tries, eventually successfully, to get the glue bottle from Hari. The repetitive language of challenge that Kevin and Jason used between themselves in play with one another at the beginning then gets turned on Hari.

Kevin: Would you think Hari would beat me?
Jason: No.
Kevin: Would you think he (*meaning some other child at the table, maybe Sean*) would beat him?
Jason: Yea.
Kevin: I'm faster than Hari. (FN 5/26/97: 10)

Here, Hari is constructed as one without prowess and therefore as not worthy. As with the teasing incident in January, Hari is constructed through the interchange between the two boys. Despite being physically present, he serves as the object of their talk and remains outside of the exchange. He cannot join in this dialogue. He leaves, has his work checked, comes back to the table to clean up, and goes over to the carpet to play cars.

Additional examples from the end of the year show that 'degradation ceremonies' constructing Hari as not welcome continue to the end of the year.

Jason: Hey, whoever wants to play cars with, whoever wants to play cars with me, put up their hands. (*Children calling 'me, me'*).

...

Jason:	Do you Casey, want to play cars with me?
Casey:	Yea:
Jason:	Hari, you can't. Do you want to, Casey?
Casey:	Yea: Hari can.
Jason:	I don't want [him to
Casey:	[Hari can.
Casey:	You have to::
Casey:	Hari's on the Jason team, right Marc?
Marc:	(... so)
Casey:	So, he has to play.
...	(Transcript, 6/9/97)

In this incident in June, the children are sitting at the table making a bee out of construction paper. Jason is calling for volunteers to play cars with him after they finish. Jason invites Casey to play with him, and he explicitly rejects Hari. During this time, Hari works quietly on his craft activity. Casey defends Hari and tries to secure him a place, repeatedly resisting the other boys' attempts to exclude Hari. However, Casey is unsuccessful.

The boys continue to do their work; shortly after, when Casey reminds Hari not to forget to put the antenna on his bee, Hari engages him in repetitive language play involving the word antenna:

Casey:	Don't forget about the antenna.
Hari:	Antinna, antinna.
Casey:	Antenna, right?
Hari:	Yea, an tenna an tenna.
Casey:	Yea, what about Antanthany?
	(*The two boys go back and forth in language play about Anthony*).

By shifting the discourse through repetitive play, Hari reinforces his affiliation with Casey at a critical time, because Jason in the preceding exchange had made an affiliating bid to Casey in the invitation to play. By his linguistic play, Hari can regain security and position himself more powerfully than in the previous interaction.

Attaining a more powerful status seems to be a perpetual struggle for Hari in the table setting, however. In the next week, I recorded the following interaction at the table:

Allan:	I'm the boss, right?
Child:	Who's second?
Hari:	I
Allan:	No::

Hari:	Yea::
Allan:	No, I the boss. You have to tell, if you see my sister, you have to tell us where she is.
Hari:	I will tell.
Allan:	That that's what your job is.
Hari:	And I'll tell.
Allan:	Yea but you're not first boss.
Hari:	Ha?
Allan:	You're not first boss.
Hari:	I'm second boss.
Allan:	You're not second boss either.
Hari:	I'm second boss.
Allan:	You're not (sixth) boss.
Hari:	I'm, I'm
Allan (?):	You're tenth boss.
Hari:	Ha? (Transcript, 6/17/97)

In this incident, Allan finally assigns Hari what one might surmise to be lowest rank: 'You're tenth boss.' Although he previously has tried to claim higher status, Hari seems to have little choice in this instance but to accept the position he is offered. Just as he had in the 'degradation' incident in January, he can only ask for clarification.

Discussion

Contemporary sociocultural researchers (e.g., Matusov, 1996; Smolka *et al.*, 1995) observe that social relations among children are very complex and have sociopolitical dimensions that learning researchers have previously rarely recognized. Lave and Wenger (1991) stress the importance of analyzing political and social organization, and the historical development of communities of practice, and their effects on ongoing learning possibilities. In their view, learning involves the construction of identity, and identity, knowing, and social membership entail one another.

Hari establishes relationships with some of his classmates during the year. Initially, he affiliates with an anglophone boy, Kevin, who sometimes seems to be helpful in easing Hari's access to and participation in the community, particularly in the beginning months of school. Hari's relationship with Kevin is dynamic and variable. Kevin supports and assists Hari in interactions with others and may even give him an 'in' to them. However, he also rebuffs Hari and affiliates with other classmates, explicitly denying any similarity with Hari ('I don't want to be like him'). He also sometimes tries to control and subordinate Hari; however, Hari sometimes can resist this positioning by setting up counter-discourse. Sometimes his resistance appears unsuccessful.

Although Hari learns that some oral practices around the table are playful and humorous (e.g., 'I put ... in here'), he also learns that there are other more unpleasant practices involving degradation (McDermott, 1993), either directly or indirectly through teasing. Hari tries to resist this positioning by setting up a repetitive counter-claim, in which he refuses to report or repeat the insult. By claiming knowledge as his own and holding onto it, he attempts to position himself as equally powerful as the other boys. He cannot win, however, because his more expert classmates have other forms of insult that they can use ('weird'). Realizing perhaps that he cannot gain control through language, Hari finally initiates a counter-challenge with a material resource which helps diffuse the situation.[3]

Despite his attempts at resistance, Hari learns that the opportunities for him to gain control and have status as a legitimate speaker are not available for him with one of the subcommunities in his class. This is particularly clear in the case of the language games, where his contributions are not productive, in that they are not continued by the other children. In the example I provided, Hari makes an innovative contribution which could in fact extend the game, but he is ignored.

According to Bakhtin, innovation in language constitutes one means by which speakers can exercise their individual voices and challenge the status quo (Hall, 1993a, 1993b, 1995). In her study of the practice of gossiping among Dominican women, Hall (1993b) shows how one woman's creative deployment of language enabled her to gain social power and transform the social order. When he creatively orchestrates a pretend reading session with other children, Hari seems very much like the successful speaker Hall describes in her study. Yet when he uses language creatively in the language game, he does not gain a place with the children he is with. As Bourdieu (1977, 1991) argues, we must look to the symbolic power relations among speakers to understand the difference.

Bourdieu (1977, 1991) theorizes that we operate with an unconscious sense of the social spaces in which we interact. He places great importance on our initial experiences where we learn the value accorded both to our linguistic productions and to our body. He also warns us that we orient our speech not so much according to linguistic expectations but rather by our chances of reception. The cumulative evidence indicates that Hari is positioned as not strong and not desirable, particularly by the more powerful boys in the class, including Kevin. Perhaps because of his positioning, Hari rarely participates in the conversational talk at the tables. He does not relate stories or personal information about himself or join in the narratives of others. The early assistance Kevin provided in hooking Hari into the multi-party talk in the fall that was so promising does not become fruitful. Hari's reticence in this area contrasts with the data for the other English language learners in the class, who all produced examples of narrative appropriations and personal narratives.

Lave and Wenger (1991) stress that personal storytelling can act as a major medium for the transformation of identity in communities of practice. Other researchers (e.g., Bruner, 1990; Miller & Goodnow, 1995; Pavlenko & Lantolf, 2000) hypothesize that narrative plays a centrally important role in constructing the self. One can thus understand that Hari might not engage in this kind of activity when the self presented to him by others is not desirable.

Many researchers (e.g., Cummins, 1996, 2000; Norton & Toohey, 2001; Siegal, 1996) remind us that language learners actively negotiate their identities in the many and varied relationships and practices they encounter. We have seen that Hari reveals a different identity in different social networks and in different oral practices. Sometimes, particularly in conjunction mainly with other girl English language learners, Hari finds he can lead and have his contributions repeated. He assumes a more powerful identity in these situations and learns that he can be at the same time challenging and communal. Hari may in these instances be experiencing a link between maleness and power. That he may do so with girls who are English language learners I find disturbing in view of his status in the boys' subcommunity and research showing how gender is socially constructed in classrooms (Davies, 1989, 1993).

According to Urwin (1984), children take up different and shifting positions within different practices. Hari's active positioning in the rhyme and story activities is consistent with this. Urwin also states that children may be active in shifting the discourse from one in which they are less powerful into another in which they are positioned more powerfully. In her study of African-American children at play in their neighborhoods, Goodwin (1990) shows how children can transform the social order of the moment by invoking a different speech activity. Maclean (1996) also shows this in his study of Grade 1 Australian children at recess time. In the interchange where he was being subordinated by some of his classmates, Hari shifted the discourse to language play with his friend Casey and succeeded in momentarily changing the social order in favor of himself. However, in the instance when he tried to verbally enter into and continue a language game, he was not successful in engaging the children's attention or continuing the game. The others shifted to propositional talk among themselves.

Hari shifted the discourse again, using his work ('Look mine') to mediate between himself and his social world.

Summary

I showed the complexity and variability of Hari's relations with his peers and the critical role they played in the identities he could negotiate and the kinds of access, participation, and opportunities for language learning that he could have. In some situations Hari was positioned as not strong and lower in status, particularly by the more powerful boys in his class. Hari had strategies for resisting the positions he was offered, but these were not always effective. Clearly, Hari did not have the power to impose recognition from some of his classmates; this situation did not change in the course of the year. This seemed to have constricted his participation and he did little to claim spaces in conversational interactions.

Notes

1. By way of comparison, Norton Peirce (1995) describes how one of her subjects, Eva, felt marginalized at her workplace and participated little in the talk there in the beginning months. After several months, however, she began to 'claim spaces in conversation with co-workers' and used personal narration to transform her position there. This occurred, according to Norton Peirce, when her conception of herself changed and when she began to see herself 'as a multicultural citizen with the power to impose reception' (p. 24)
2. Childen rapidly creating a chain of 'I likes' (pointing and moving their fingers away) is a common playful oral practice observed in this classroom.
3. Sociocultural theorists urge us to look not on the individual alone but on the individual-operating-with-mediational means. This example shows how Hari's sign differs according to the mediational means employed (i.e., language vs. material object).

Chapter 6
Hari and Casey, a Newcomer

> ... language, for the individual consciousness, lies on the borderline between oneself and the other. The word in language is half someone else's. It becomes 'one's own' only when the speaker populates it with his own intention, his own accent, when he appropriates the word, adapting it to his own semantic and expressive intention.
>
> (Bakhtin, 1981: 293)

At the end of the previous chapter, I described one incident when Hari strategically reinforced his affiliation with a child named Casey ('Don't forget about the antenna'), who had just tried to secure Hari a place with the others. In this chapter, I trace the development of Hari's relationship with Casey, who was a newcomer to the class in late January. I analyze social and political aspects of their relationship, but I focus more closely on questions of identity and language appropriation, structuring my analysis around the following question:

What is the quality of Hari's relationship with Casey and how does this affect possibilities for learning?

In the first section, I examine the two pupils' interactions in the table and circle settings and the roles and kinds of identity positions open to Hari therein. In the second section, I examine the activity time sessions between Hari and Casey, focusing on questions of participation, access, and identity. In the third section, I examine subsequent activity time sessions to further understand the kinds of positions on offer to Hari, the identities available to him and how these affected his possibilities for appropriating language.

Casey is an anglophone boy who first joined the class in late January. My field notes indicate that he seemed quite 'squirrelly' in the first few months in the classroom and that it took him a while to settle into its smooth disciplinary routine. In my observations of him in February and March, I noted that Mrs Clark called him to task for various 'unruly' behaviors (e.g., talking in circle, playing around with scissors, etc.), once showing a rare hint of annoyance ('Mrs Clark reprimands Casey. She seems annoyed. Casey the one who hasn't been absorbed fully into her community yet?' FN

3/4/97: 9). By late March, however, I noted that she no longer seemed to have to do this (FN 3/26/97: 4).

Casey seemed to find a way into the life of the classroom fairly soon after his arrival. I observed him initiating playful non-verbal interactions with some of the children in the circle in mid-February:

> Casey jabs Anita. She smiles, jabs him back.... (Note: Jabbing a way of becoming familiar?) After kids move into circle for mail distribution, Casey moves close to Joanna. She pats his shoulders, then his running shoes. (FN 2/19/97: 16)

When he arrived, Casey chose to sit at the long table where the other boys, including Hari, often congregated for work and craft activities and for lunch, and his preference for this location remained constant throughout the year. Casey began to join in the table talk among the children early on, as the following excerpt from my field notes shows:

Jason: (*to Casey*) You were a baby when you came out of your mom's stomach....
Thomas: (*turning toward their end of the table and joining in*) With the blood inside.
Casey: You're born naked. (FN 2/13/97: 7)

Indeed, in my observations of Casey over the year, I found it remarkable how he managed to gain and maintain a position as a respected and legitimate speaker at the table and could impose reception in ways that Hari could not. The field notes and transcripts contain many examples of conversations he had with the other children:

Kevin: You know what, I was begging and begging my mom.
Child: ...
Casey: I keep on telling her and telling her: get a present for Casey, get a present for Casey.
Child: Because my ... (Transcript, 5/1/97)

At the same time as he managed to develop what seemed to me to be comfortable relations with some of the other children in the class, Casey also developed a relationship with Hari, often sitting near him at the tables and spending activity time with him.

Social Relations

I first began to observe Hari and Casey sitting by one another in the morning circle and interacting with one another at the long table in mid-February. In late February (2/25/97), I recorded the following conversation at snack time:

Casey: Know wha:t? One day ah my friend named Christopher at at school, at at my old school, my friend named Christopher's at at his old school, when there was a sticker on the apple, when he was having it for lunch and then he ate the sticker on the apple. He ate the sticker (*pause*) yea:
Child: It can't be true.
Casey: It is.
Child: (...)
Hari: Yea, and when you eat the sticker you, you think to that he ... (Transcript, 2/25/97)

In this instance, Casey initiates a conversation using, as the children frequently do, the food they are eating as a point of departure. Casey tells a narrative on the basis of the apple he is eating and Hari joins in with a comment. Later, I noticed the two boys playfully kicking one another (FN 2/25/97: 17).

Some of the table interactions between the two boys during February suggest that Hari takes on an old-timer role with Casey.[1] For example, he explains to Casey about the cutting and pasting they are doing, telling him that he also does it in the afternoon, '... even you can do it in the afternoon class' (FN 2/18/97: 9). He also uses an old-timer practice to initiate a playful interaction with Casey as they are sitting at the long table cutting out from catalogues:

Hari points his finger to a picture in Casey's catalogue, saying 'I like this one,' then moves his fingers quickly away. Sue joins in: 'I like this one,' pointing to a picture and quickly moving her fingers away. (FN 2/18/97: 9)

Also, Hari initiates Casey into an item of classroom culture, pointing out a table mate's 'hot dog,' and showing him the movements to a favorite classroom song which involves wiggling to the words 'hot dog' (FN 2/25/97: 17).

As these examples show, Hari is an old-timer with respect to some of the classroom practices. However, he seems to be a newcomer with respect to other practices and can appeal to Casey for an audience when his attempts at participation are ignored. On one occasion, for example, many of the boys are in the carpeted area looking in catalogues for pictures to cut out and are pointing out pictures of women in underwear to one another. Hari observes them, seems partially to figure out what they are doing, and tries to join in. He looks through his catalogue, finds a picture of a woman in a dress, and points to it calling, 'Jason, lookit.' Jason ignores him, not even looking at what Hari is pointing to, and so Hari tries to show the picture to Casey, who is working at the long table: 'Casey, Casey, lookit.' Casey is diverted by the teacher (FN 2/18/97: 9).

The incident shows that Hari does not gain an audience when he tries to make sense of and participate in a classroom practice with which he seems unfamiliar. When the others do not respond to his attempt at participation, Hari perceives that Casey, as a newcomer to the classroom at large, might provide an alternate audience to whom he can appeal.[2]

In my observations, I also saw Casey establishing relations with some of the other children in the classroom: for example, gesturing and talking with Kevin in the circle and spending activity time with him in early March. However, I also continued to observe occasions on which Hari and Casey were in proximity to one another at the long table and in the circle throughout March. In addition, I observed the two boys with one another during activity time for the first time in mid-March (3/12/97) and several times after this. I will discuss their activity time play in a later section; here, I examine some of their interactions in the table and circle settings during the rest of the school year in order to show the development of their relationship and the kinds of identity positions open to Hari within it.

In April, I noticed a qualitative change in some of the interactions between Hari and Casey. On some occasions, Casey provides Hari with a chance to play the role of master or expert with respect to their classroom work. For example, in early April, he asks Hari to help him draw a monkey: 'Can you draw a monkey? I don't know how to draw a monkey.' Hari takes a brown crayon from the tub and draws a monkey, verbalizing as he demonstrates to Casey, 'And hands and feet brown. A monkey is brown' (FN 4/9/97: 14). This example suggests that Casey recognizes his classmate as having expertise in some domains. The following examples show that Casey also brings this expertise forth.

In April, I observed Casey encouraging Hari in his growing expertness in reading. As Hari returns to the circle after having read the first line of the reading message, Casey calls out to him, 'Next time read the whole thing, okay?' (FN 4/23/97), projecting an image of him as a capable reader. Hari does indeed grow to read the entire reading message, and in early June, I noticed that Hari smiles at Casey as he returns to the circle after having done so (FN 6/9/97: 4).

Casey also brings forth Hari's expertness by imagining the possibilities in Hari's work. Once in early May (5/1/97), Hari, Casey, Claudia, and Paula were sitting at the table making chicks out of construction paper. To do this, they had to cut triangles out of the paper. Hari has cut out several triangles and holds up his sheet:

Hari:	(*holding up his sheet of paper*) Look garbage.
Casey:	(*to Claudia*) Look it, look at what Hari made! Look at what Hari made! Claudia, look what Hari made.
	(*addressing Hari*) Open it up.
Hari:	Triangle.
Casey:	See look.
Hari:	I, I, I just making triangle (…) hat (…) hat (…) the hat. What all is done (*background voices*) I, I did it. (Transcript, 5/1/97)

Thus, Casey notices that Hari's sheet of paper looks like a birthday (or party) hat, calls it to Claudia's attention and encourages Hari to open it up, giving him a chance to explain how he did it (FN 5/1/97: 6).

As we saw in the previous chapter, Casey also supports Hari. In this example, Hari shows Casey his drawing, enthusiastically pointing out the many colors in it:

Hari:	(*with rounded gestures as if to make a rainbow, shows Casey his drawing*) There got lots of colors=
Casey:	=yea
Hari:	Brown, black
Casey:	(*points to drawing and says to Hari*) But there's, but there isn't brown.
Jason:	(*laughing*) (…) look at Hari.
Casey:	(*to Jason*) He likes colors, he likes colors.
Jason:	(*laughing*) Haw haw haw haw haw keeee ew. (Transcript, 5/12/97 and FN 5/12/97: 7)

Though not hesitating to correct him on one of the colors, Casey looks at Hari's drawing approvingly. While Jason laughs, not showing too much appreciation for Hari's colorful drawing, Casey comments approvingly, seeming to defend Hari from any potential criticism: 'He likes colors, he likes colors.'

Finally, Casey supports Hari in subtle ways. One morning, after Mrs Clark has introduced a verse about butterflies, Hari volunteers:

Hari:	I saw a butterfly in my house.
Teacher:	Did you? What color was it?
Child:	(...) back door.
Teacher:	And what color was it, Hari?
Hari:	White.
Teacher:	A white one

...

Claudia:	I saw one but it was yellow.
Casey:	I saw one but it was white. (Transcript, 5/26/97)

Hari tells the teacher that he saw a butterfly, which was white. When Claudia says she saw a yellow butterfly, Casey repeats her frame, substituting the color 'white' for 'yellow,' thus reinforcing Hari's observation.

In summary, these data show that Hari's relationship with Casey positions him as worthy and encourages his identity as a master. Over time, Hari and Casey's relationship seemed to me to take on the quality of a friendship. The data presented above reflect this developing alliance. Other indications, such as affective gestures (e.g., waving, saving a spot in the circle 5/26/97) and their repeated and prolonged engagement in activity time together over the course of the year also suggest they are becoming friends, at least in the classroom.

Participation

In examining the activity time sessions between Hari and Casey, I focus on what kinds of access Hari has, how he participates, and what identities he can negotiate with Casey. I first observed Hari and Casey at activity time together in mid-March (FN 3/12/97). Before this, I saw Casey at the computer during activity time, alone or in the company of other children. In early March, I observed him playing trains with Kevin and Sean (FN 3/4/97: 2). During this time period, I saw Hari once at the computer, briefly with Casey, and once briefly at the sand table with Sean (FN 2/10/97: 8). However, Hari mainly played alone during activity time, either doing a craft activity or playing with Playmobil or Lego (FN 2/18/97; FN 2/25/97; FN 3/4/97).

My field notes for the activity time in which Hari and Casey first come to play together also show that Hari is at first playing alone, this time with little toy motorcycles (FN 3/12/97: 11). Perhaps to avoid being alone, he makes some initiatives to others in the area. First, he shows his dirt bike to Thomas and Marc ('This is a dirt bike'; 'Hey, little bike'), who are together on the carpet, copying and printing the letters assigned for the day. They ignore him, engrossed in their work. Then he scoots around with his dirt bike to the other end of the carpet and makes overtures to Jason and Allan, who are there playing with tracks, but they ignore him; Hari returns to his area of the carpet. As if to fill the gap, Casey walks over to Hari and asks if he can play. Hari accepts.

The two boys then engage in amicable play with the dirt bikes. The following two excerpts from the transcript show how they negotiate resources and terminology:[3]

Hari:	Yea, you can have this dirt bike after (...) this is my motor-cycle, dirt bike.
Casey:	That is racing bike, okay?
Hari:	1, 2, 3, 4.
Casey:	I'm this car.
Hari:	Here's a dirt bike, then, here's a dirt bike. You want it? (*gives Casey a bike*)
Casey:	I'll have this one.
Hari:	Okay, mine is good, rrm vrrrrr.
Casey:	Dirt bikes go in the dirt, dirt bikes ride in the dirt, that's why they're called dirt bikes.
...	
Casey:	The dirt bike, yea: (you're going) on the motorcycle.
Hari:	Look my moto motorcycle.
Casey:	You mean dirt bike?
Hari:	Yea, your is race bike.
Casey:	Yea, I'm racing it.
Hari:	I'm this dirt bike.
Casey:	Then you have to ride in the dirt. (Transcript, 3/12/97)

They also negotiate tasks. As the following excerpt shows, Hari success-fully maintains his position, through insisting on putting a little toy helmet on Casey's dirt bike rider.

Hari:	(*gives him a little toy helmet. Casey tries to put it on his dirt bike person*) I can put it on.
Casey:	(*trying to put it on*) ... I can do that.
Hari:	I do it.
...	

(*Casey finally gives it to him and Hari puts it on. As Hari does so, Casey says, 'I'll do it.' Hari finishes putting it on and gives it to Casey, saying, 'Here it is' ['pronounced 'diz']. FN 3/12/97: 12*)

In the ensuing play, the transcript (not included here) shows that Hari can have a productive role in the play. He insists, 'I gotta go to your home,' adds his own innovations to the game ('Me too, and somebody drive my car, this guy…. '), riding his vehicle where he wants, and putting more people in it ('And I got two people to ride'). Hari also counters Casey, as the following excerpt shows:

Hari: Look, I got the ne:::w car.
Casey: Well, I got a new boat, well, I got a boat.
Hari: You have not new boat. I got a ne::w birthday boat. He::y, you wanna ride it? This is number 1 (guy). You gonna (keep) some pieces on dirt bike, my number 1 (guy). Hey, you wanna race it off?
Casey: Look, I'll ride it and then I'll g, I have to go to carry bu:d, vrrrrr[rrrrr
Hari: [wait for me:
Casey: And remember, it's right near the water is (…)

Hari also inserts his own pretend interjection: 'Pretend that we go here. I wanna go.' But Casey replies, 'No::, this is the water, you can't swim that fast.'

Soon afterwards, Casey leads the play. Casey uses several 'pretend' interjections and dialogue directives ('Bud, don't do it'), which Hari sometimes accepts and repeats:

Casey: Hey pretend these were in the water and you're going to watch me do a jump and pretend you said, 'Bud, don't do it, bud, don't do it, bud' (*crashing sounds*). Say, 'Bud, don't do it.'
Hari: Bud, don't do: it (*pause*) Bud, don't do it.
Casey: Now I go in the water, this is the water.
Hari: Vrrrrrrr.
              (*sounds of kids, cars crashing*)
Hari: Don't do: it, bu:d.

However, while Casey is dominant, the following excerpts illustrate that Hari makes independent decisions about his role in this pretend game ('I'm not bud'; 'I coming in the wa::::::'); he also makes additions to the pretend game ('And hurt my guy, you … in the trouble').

Casey: Come on, get out. Pretend this was my boat. This was nobody else's boat except for mine, okay?
Hari: I, I just get out and [(…)
Casey: [Bud, don't get in my boat.
Hari: You're were just looking (…)

Casey:	Pretend you're pretending to drive it 'cause you were just here.
…	
	(*rrrrrrrrrr*)
…	
Casey:	Bud, get off my boat.
Hari:	I'm not bud.
…	
Hari:	Look, hey, look, my motorcycle bike (tires). Look, this broken.
Casey:	BlllllllllllllllllII
Hari:	[Hey, there is (in) the water. I coming in the wa::::::: (*rising intonation*)
Casey:	Blllllllll hey, know what I did, watch this. Know what I did, blllllllll ah:: you're coming in the water, move it back in the water::::
Hari:	Hey, my motorcycle bike.
…	
Casey:	Okay, (…) pretend I sh, pretend I shot it right at the side head and he got knocked out, do: oo::. Oops, and pretend you went ah:, you gonna be dea:d (*pause*) because I knocked him out.
Hari:	And hurt my guy. You in (*pause*) you in in the trouble, in the trouble.

At the end of activity time, the two boys clean up. When Hari starts to pick up the bucket, Casey wants to carry it. Hari picks it up and proposes to Casey that they carry it together, one on each side: 'You carry this and I carry this.' The two boys go off together, doing as Hari had proposed (FN 3/12/97: 14). Hari's success in having this cooperative initiative accepted is a contrast to his experiences with some of his other peers, who, according to my observations, pay no attention to his cooperative initiatives and succeed at dominating.

In this car-playing episode, Hari maintains active participation throughout. Casey gives him words (e.g., 'Say, "Bud, don't do it"'), and Hari sometimes accepts and repeats these. There is ongoing negotiation between the two boys with respect to language, resources, power relations, and identity positions. As we saw in the previous chapter, there was little or no room for such negotiation in the car-playing episode in the fall, when Kevin tried to control the play and Hari resisted by folding his arms, refusing to talk or to play.

Appropriation

Hari and Casey played together during activity time frequently during the rest of the year, often spending the whole activity period together playing cars or, in a few cases, board games and other activities. Such activities, particularly car-playing, helped to understand the kinds of positions the relationship offered to Hari, the identities it made available to him, and the possibilities it gave him for appropriating language and taking on his own perspective or voice. As I observed the two playing cars, I was struck with how frequently Casey initiated pretend frames and with how accepting of these Hari was. I had observed Hari playing cars in the afternoon class with one of his Punjabi-speaking peers and had noticed them changing their voices and using dialogue without the mediation of a pretend frame and dialogue directives such as those given by Casey.

	(Baldev and Hari wheeling cars along carpet, speaking in dialogue)
Baldev:	Sister, can you go in the back?
Hari:	*(bypassing Baldev with his car)* Hey, friend, I don't want to hit you.
Baldev:	*(going along the line of the carpet with his car)* But can you follow me? (FN 2/6/97: 6)

This interaction suggested to me a more equal balance of roles than in the pretend play with Casey, where I thought that Casey might be dominating and keeping Hari in a subordinate role. So I had a particular interest in further examining the data for activity time in order to explore the nature of Hari and Casey's relationship.

The field notes and recordings for the car-playing sessions in April and May show similar features as the car-playing episode in March. As in other car-playing sessions, Casey frequently makes pretend interjections and tries to establish a structure and script for the play. In this way, he seems to be inviting Hari to enter his world and share his perspective on the play. Hari can move fluidly in and out of Casey's pretend frames; there is reciprocity in the car-playing activity. The following excerpts from a transcript at the end of May (5/26/97) illustrate some of the play dialogue between the two boys:

Hari:	*(driving a car on its side)* Look at I'm driving on <u>two</u> wheels. *(The two boys drive their cars along the carpet).*
Casey:	We can't hear you. We can't, I can't hear you because you're inside your ca:r, vrrrrrrrr[rr.
Hari:	[I open a window.
Casey:	Vrrrr, arrrrrrr, and you said, 'Who's parked in my <u>ho:me</u>?'

Hari:	Who's parking in my <u>ho:me</u>?
Casey:	And know what? ....
	(*rrrrrrrrrrrrr*)
Hari:	(Here) Hey bud, what you doing?
Casey:	<u>No</u> I'm not your bud, and you said, 'Who took my (driver).'
Hari:	(Who ... my driver)
...	
Casey:	... So I went into the water and you said, 'Bu:d, bu:d watch ou:t' (...) and you was gonna go in the water, and when you went in the water, you jumped in the water and then I came out. Go in the wa:ter. And I came out. Don't come out! Don't come out! You didn't see me. Hey now I got (...)
Hari:	Rrrrrrrr rrrr
Casey:	But you don't leave your island. You live right here.
Hari:	I crashing. I crashing, rrrrrr. (Transcript, 5/26/97)

Hari sometimes accepts the frames and sometimes repeats the words Casey gives him. He also inserts his own inventions in the play (e.g., 'I crashing').

In the ensuing play, Casey points to a corner of the carpet where he wants Hari to be stationed, but Hari ignores his friend's directives and decides to live in the opposite corner. As can be seen, Hari takes over the game with his favored conversational opener 'Don't you know.' When he does so, it is interesting that Casey changes his formulation of the pretend script from himself to Hari as the originator of the words ('And pretend you said: Bud look ... Pretend you said, "Hey Hari says, 'Bud look out'"'). Hari repeats with the same intonation as Casey, 'Bud look out.' And he continues with his own inventions, 'Don't you know....'

Casey:	Know what I did, watch, good, I'm almost away from him, and you said, 'Get him, bud' and I went like this, and he said, 'Ah psh::: pshhhh::: pshhhh::: rrrr rrr[rr.'
Hari:	[Don't you know, I was (smashing over) to him and the (roller) too and um don't you know (... [.)
Casey:	[And pretend you said: Bu:::d look
Hari:	Rrrrrrrr[rr
Casey:	[Pretend you said, 'Hey Hari says: "Bu:d, look out::."'
Hari:	Bu:d, look out:: *(same intonation as Casey)*
Casey:	And I fell in the water.
Hari:	Don't you know, rrrr rrrrr vrr[rr.
Casey:	[eeeah pyew

Hari: Rrrr rrrr rrrr aaah
Casey: Is that you?
Hari: No this is me.
Casey: That's you?

The interchange shows how in their play the two boys pass the role of conversational initiator and director back and forth.[4] Hari establishes his version of the pretend world by claiming a different physical space, and he takes the right to speak with the linguistic marker 'Don't you know.' Casey accepts this and gives Hari ownership of the words ('Pretend you said, "Hey Hari says: 'Bud look out'"').

As the two boys continue to play cars, Eva, another English language learner, is standing in the area. She makes an overture to them, showing them the puzzle she has done. On this occasion, the boys momentarily look at Eva's puzzle, but then return to their car-playing:

Casey: Hari
Hari: I know how to (…) eenie meenie minie moe=
                (The two boys are moving their cars along the tracks. Casey joins in with Hari).
**Hari
and Casey:**   *(together)* =let the tiger by
                the toe who hollers let him go, eenie, meenie, minie, moe *(said with rhythmic beat and somewhat louder voices).*

As they move their cars along the tracks, Hari starts an 'eenie, meenie, minie, moe' rhyme, which I had earlier heard being bandied about in the classroom. Casey joins him, and they continue the rhyme together. As in the incident in the previous chapter where Hari shifted the discourse to language play in order to affiliate with Casey, these two boys shifted almost unconsciously, it appeared to me, to the rhyme and coordinated each other rhythmically. This shift in discourse seems to be a way to help them reestablish the activity and in the process demarcate them from this girl (or reestablish the activity as it was without the girl).

Later, Eva returns and again makes overtures to them, but they ignore her and she leaves:

Casey: Brrrrrr brrrrrr drrrrdrrrr rrrrrrrr, I'm the boss of the road
Hari: Look [it, I'm the cool guy
Casey: [Ba pa pa pa, ba pa pa pa, ba pa pa pa, ba pa pa pa, ba pa pa pa pa pa ba pa pa *(rising voice)* *(Hari going along to the beat, can be heard in background, but not with the clear sounds like Casey)* ba pa pa pa *(rising voice)*. (Transcript, 5/26/97)

The two boys break out into language play, which reinforces their affiliation. Though this snub is very unfortunate for Eva, the incident shows how much Hari and Casey come to form one unit through their play and how their language play reinforces this.

The reciprocity and momentary unity in Hari's and Casey's interactions contrasts strikingly with the interactions between Hari and the other boys at activity time. Although I sometimes saw Hari with the other boys at activity time, they were mostly engaged in parallel play; Hari's interactions with them concern allocation of space (e.g., Hari: 'I can play over there at that mat.' Kevin: 'I can play on this mat'; FN 4/9/97: 14).

More commonly these interactions concern allocation of resources. In one incident, Hari has a shiny red racing car, which Kevin claims is his (Kevin to Hari: 'How many cars did you take?' … 'Hari, you took that car from me. You should ask'; FN 4/9/97: 15–16). Allan suggests that they appeal to Mrs Clark, and Casey, noticing that there is a problem, comes over and proposes a solution: 'We'll throw the car into the junk.' Kevin tries to get the coveted car back by offering Hari a different red racing car, but this doesn't seem to work, and so he threatens to tell the teacher and accuses Hari of taking all his cars. Hari proposes an amicable solution, allowing Kevin to take the coveted car first: 'No, you play it, then me play it, then you play it.' They exchange cars, with Kevin getting the coveted car, but when Hari later claims his turn at the car ('I want that please, please, please'), Kevin does not give it up.

Field notes and transcripts for other activity times during the year show that Hari's interactions with the other boys also concern allocation of space and resources and do not involve interactive play. In the following example, Hari is setting up on one car mat, Jason and Allan on another. The car bucket is between the two car mats.

> Jason takes a car from Hari's area. Hari bunches all the cars up with his hands to keep them. In retaliation, he goes over to their rug and gets a car from their set up. The boys resolve all this by trading cars. Hari holds up a green car and says, 'Hey, look; I got a nice car.' Jason grabs a car again. Hari bunches up the cars with his hands, grabs a car from Allan's rug. Casey comes over and asks Hari if he can play. (FN 5/6/97: 12)

This particular incident seems amicable, indeed playful. But it does not open up avenues to the kind of reciprocal play dialogue in which Hari and Casey engage. In the previous chapter, we saw how Hari was not accepted as a legitimate speaker of the others' words. Here, he is positioned in the role of impostor and illegitimate taker of the others' resources.

Discussion

Rogoff (1990) emphasizes the importance of a variety of social relation-ships to children because such variety provides them with opportunities to participate in diverse roles. Additionally, she points out that it also may serve to overcome social difficulties encountered. Hari took on the role of old-timer when Casey first arrived and could appeal to him as an alterna-tive audience in a situation when his attempts at participation in one of the boys' practices were ignored. As time went by, Casey provided Hari with the chance to take on the role of master or expert with respect to their school work, asking Hari to assist him, encouraging Hari's growing expertness, and even metaphorically bringing it into being. For example, the incidents where Casey encouraged Hari to 'next time read the whole thing' and brought Hari's drawing of a hat into being seem to be a kind of prolepsis, described by Cole as 'the representation of a future act or development as being presently existing' (Cole, 1996: 183).

Overall, I showed that Hari's relationship with Casey positioned him as worthy and encouraged his identity as a master or expert, and gave support to his utterances. Children ratifying one another's speech has frequently been observed in this kindergarten classroom and in other class-rooms (Toohey, 1998) and seems to be one of the 'subtle processes' through which James *et al.* (1998) have argued that friendship in children is enacted. Consequently, I noted that the two boys' relationship seemed to take on the quality of a friendship.[5]

My interpretation is supported by Rizzo's (1989) research on friendship development among children in school. Rizzo notes that three of the most frequently indexed dimensions of friendship are helping, sharing, and work-related ego-reinforcement, which he describes as 'bolstering the self-esteem or prestige of one's friend by showing an appreciation for their achievements, products, or possessions' (p. 119).

However, I would like here to emphasize that, although his work has helped confirm my interpretation, some of Rizzo's classifications (e.g., 'work related ego-reinforcement') cannot do justice to the quality of the two boys' interactions and what these may have meant to Hari, especially in the context of some of his other experiences in the class. Dewey (1989) writes of some of the dangers of classifying and categorizing: 'A classified and hierarchically ordered set of pluralities, of variants, has none of the sting of the miscellaneous and uncoordinated plurals of our actual world' (p. 49). Neither will it have any of the pleasure. Although the interactions in the previous chapter showed some of the 'sting' of the particulars of these children's lives, some of the interactions in the present chapter also remind us of their beauty.

The political theorist Bourdieu argues that we should see friendship, like language and education, as a symbolic resource to which access is critical (Carrington & Luke, 1997). As Norton (2000) explains, it is through participation in social networks that one gains access to power and privilege which influence one's sense of self or identity. In activity-time sessions with Casey, Hari participated actively throughout and there was ongoing negotiation between the two boys with respect to language, resources, power relations, and identity positions, unlike Hari's relations with the other boys. Bakhtin's (1981) distinction between authoritative and internally persuasive discourse helps characterize the nature of the differences observed and understand the kind of participation allowed.[6] In authoritative discourse, someone assumes a position of authority over other speakers and allows these others no opportunity to play in the text. Internally persuasive discourse, by contrast, is open to the interanimation of other voices and engenders spontaneity, risk-taking and creativity. Clearly, Hari's and Casey's relationship allows for internally persuasive discourse. Toohey and Day (1999) illustrated how situations of internally persuasive discourse fostered English language learners' participation and appropriation of voice by allowing them to find desirable identities in words and to answer back and play in the words of others around them.

Bakhtin (1981, 1986) argues that individual consciousness is intersubjective and is realized in our interactions with others. He envisages the constitution of self as an ongoing process involving struggle between the self and other. He also sees learning language as a struggle in which we appropriate others' words and make them our own by adopting our own perspective.

During the car-playing, Casey sometimes explicitly directs the dialogue, and Hari sometimes repeats the same utterance. Casey also directs the play, but Hari too can take over; when he does, Casey accepts this and also grants Hari ownership of his own words: 'Pretend you said, "Hey Hari says: 'Bud look out.'"' Bakhtin stresses that there is struggle involved when we appropriate the words of others even with their collusion. For him, no two apparently identical utterances made by different individuals can ever be truly alike, because dialogic relations are always present when we talk:

> *Agreement* is very rich in varieties and shadings. Two utterances that are identical in all respects ('Beautiful weather!' – 'Beautiful weather!'),

if they are really *two* utterances belonging to *different* voices and not one, are linked by dialogic *relations of agreement*. This is a definite dialogic event in the interrelations of the two, and not an echo. For after all, agreement could also be lacking ('No, not very nice weather,' and so forth). (Bakhtin, 1986: 125)

In Bakhtin's conception of dialogue, the word encounters an alien word and the self encounters an alien self in tension-filled interaction. This 'dialogism' stresses that we should look to the relationship between the self and other and between one's own and others' words as a critical area where the struggle to establish oneself and one's language takes place.

In a study analyzing interview interactions involving an adult learner, Angélil-Carter (1997) shows how a learner's ability to claim the right to speak can change even within one encounter, which following Bourdieu (1991), she refers to as 'the skeptron.' Hari and Casey passed the skeptron back and forth in their play. Sometimes Hari agreed with Casey; sometimes he did not. Sometimes he appropriated Casey's words; sometimes he did not. There was ongoing negotiation in a relationship of respect and care.

When Eva, one of the English language learners, tried to gain entry, Casey initiated a shift in discourse which reinforced his and Hari's affiliation; their language became synchronized, and they formed one unit. However, although it took an outsider to provoke it, their becoming as one was perhaps only possible because of the dialectical character of the interplay that preceded it.

This affiliating language seems to be equivalent to the way I observed Hari and his L1 classmates use Punjabi a few times in the fall to create boundaries around their play. This observation corresponds with Gumperz' (1982: 208) notion of conversational contextualization, a relational signaling function, which can be played by seemingly different phenomena (e.g., code-switching, prosody, phonetic and morphological variation, choice of syntactic or lexical option).

Summary

I showed that Hari developed a respected place with his classmate, Casey, with whom he developed a friendship over the year. The activity time play of the two children showed how Hari was able to negotiate identity and linguistic and other resources on an ongoing basis in a relationship of caring, trust, and reciprocity. Hari was able to appropriate language freely and take on a voice, a place from which to speak, under conditions which did not threaten or constrain him. These conditions obtained with Casey and, as we will see in the next chapter, also with his teacher.

Notes

1. By way of comparison, in her study of the Cohort 1 kindergarten children, Toohey (1996) found that one child (Harvey), who was often excluded from other children's activities, took up with a newcomer, mentoring his involvement in classroom routines and spending some play time with him in the first month.
2. As a contrast, the reader is reminded of the incident in the previous chapter when Hari successfully gained reception and was able to affiliate with Kevin and Allan when he tried to make sense of and participate in a playful language practice ('I put Slurpy in here') at snack time.
3. For reference purposes, I have divided the transcript into sections separated by …
4. Bourdieu (1991) adopts the term 'skeptron,' which in Homer is passed to the orator next to speak in order to enjoin silence from the audience. Bourdieu argues that the skeptron concretely exemplifies the fact that authority comes to language from outside.
5. James *et al.* (1998) discuss research on friendship among young children in Great Britain showing that children may understand the word 'friend' differently from adults. It is important to recognize this in considering the relationship between the two boys.
6. In an analysis of a car-playing episode among Grade 1 students in a Punjabi-Sikh school, Toohey *et al.* (2000) showed how children negotiated power relations in play and how relations of dominance were such that they constrained participation and occasioned withdrawal.

Chapter 7

Hari and his Teacher

> What leads an individual to pursue some identities and abandon or
> ignore others? It seems that we must find some way of understanding
> how individuals actively construct their personal goals, beliefs about
> themselves, and images of self *out of* the cultural models and socializa-
> tion processes to which they are exposed.
>
> (Eisenhart, 1995: 5)

In this chapter, I take up the perspectives of researchers who have introduced psychoanalytic theories on the role of unconscious desires and identification to considerations of learning. I examine Hari's relationship and
interactions with his teacher, Mrs Clark, focusing on the following
question:

> What are the social and political dimensions of Hari's relationship with
> his teacher and how do these affect possibilities for learning?

In the first section, I consider how Hari participates in circle activities,
showing changes in the quality of participation in these settings. In the
second section, I examine the teacher's discourse, revealing her construction of Hari and her positioning of him as a student. In the final section, I
examine how Hari plays his role in maintaining and enhancing the position
that the teacher has offered to him. I close with the teacher's final evaluation of Hari's progress over the year.

Participation

Hari's teacher characterizes him as 'shy,' 'reluctant to ask for help,' and
not saying 'a word' at the beginning of the school year. His parents also
report that he was uneasy at school in the very beginning. By November,
Mrs Clark reports that his progress is fine, commenting on him in affective
tones and describing his participation as follows:

Elaine: How about Hari?
Mrs Clark: Oh I could just take him home. Oh you know some of them
just creep into your heart. I find him so so innocent.... He
certainly tries hard; he's very attentive but he tries to partici-

pate and contribute ideas and suggestions and (corrects) himself. (Teacher interview, 11/19/96)

The observational data from the first three months show that Hari occasionally contributes a one-word answer to the teacher's questions during whole group activities:

> (*Mrs Clark holds up a coloring sheet with a turkey on it*).

Teacher: ... Let's see, here's a word in this feather. It's the word for r-e-d.

Hari: Red.

Teacher: Can we find that word somewhere in the class?
Some children: Re::d.

Teacher: (*acknowledging Hari*) Right, I heard it; that's right, red. (Transcript, 10/7/96)

He also sometimes briefly addresses Mrs Clark as she circulates in the classroom. In an early observation in September, he shows his work to her after she asks him and his table mates whether they have found anything red to cut from the catalogues they are searching through:

> As Hari cuts, he says 'red' for each object cut. Raj tries to get his attention, taps his shoulder. Hari sees Mrs Clark nearby and goes to show her the red thing he has cut. Hari says: 'Teacher, I've got some red' (he has a retroflex 'r'). (FN 9/17/96: 6)

He also asks for her assistance with the craft materials and, in one instance, appeals to her in a problem with a table mate.

> Hari leans over Trevor's paper. Trevor slaps him a bit. Hari moves away a bit. A few seconds later when the teacher comes to the table to check their drawing, Hari points to Trevor and says to the teacher, 'He's fighting me.' (FN 10/16/96: 3)

Hari makes his first contribution to sharing in the circle at the end of October.

Teacher: Now let's see. I start around the circle. I guess Hari you're the first boy I come to. Do you have something you'd like to share with us today?
(*5 seconds silence*)

Hari: (*pointing to and touching floor*) My, my mom give new Batman and a (*pause*) car.

Teacher: A Batman and a car? Wow, these are new toys? for you?

Hari: No, um, mom give me.

Teacher:	She bought them at the store? Wow. Now are you still going to be the Power Ranger at Halloween? like a Power Ranger? for Halloween? It's nice mom bought you some new things. Thank you for sharing … (Transcript, 10/28/96)

Mrs Clark repeats Hari's last words and asks him if they are new toys. Hari maintains his mom as the topic, repeating, 'Mom give me.' Mrs Clark accepts and expands on this, and then tries to initiate further dialogue by talking about Halloween. When Hari does not respond, she returns to the original topic and sums up approvingly: 'It's nice mom bought you some new things.'

The teacher's acceptance of his contributions, her adeptness at building on what he says, and her encouragement of but not insistence on further talk, are scaffolding practices that assist Hari's participation. Hari contributes briefly to the circle talk again a few times in December.

	(Kim shares. Manjit raises her hand and so does Anna).
Mrs Clark:	*(to Hari)* You have one too?
Hari:	At my house. On my TV.
	(Kim shows his Power Ranger toy.) (FN 12/5/96: 2)

Hari:	*(raises his hand)* … My … he brings me little Santa.
Mrs Clark:	Wow, that's special, so the little Santa, does he hang upon the Christmas tree? (FN 12/10/96: 1)

Hari becomes significantly more active in the classroom circle in the new year, as indicated by his lengthy contributions and attempts to hold the floor. During guessing bag time in mid-January (1/13/97), he volunteers a long story about a party he had gone to. Immediately after this, he tries to maintain the floor by relating a personal narrative about a dinosaur, a topic suggested to him perhaps because a child had previously shared a guessing bag with a tyrannosaurus rex in it.

Hari:	I go in the party.
Teacher:	Oh where?
Hari:	Somebody's house and all the big boys …
	(He's speaking slowly and low. He is saying a lot more but I cannot make out what he is saying).
Teacher:	Oh so there was a stage and the big
Hari:	And me and my friend go in the party – BIG
	And then my sister and me pushed the and my friend and me
	And I drinked a coke
	So loud when …
	(He is saying lots).

And my mom too.

Teacher: Sounds like a good party.

(*Hari keeps going*).

...

Hari: A big dinosaur – come in my house – I have a small dinosaur. Then he got big.

(*Kids do not look like they're listening to him. He goes on for a couple of minutes...*).

Teacher: Oh ... Are there dinosaurs now?

Hari: But I dreamed it. I watched the TV and then I dreamed it. And I was scared. (FN 1/13/97: 1)

The dramatic increase in participation which Hari shows in mid-January is also shown in other circle activities and classroom events after this time, and this does not go unnoticed by Mrs Clark. A few days later, she spontaneously approaches me while I am observing the children seated at their tables drawing a brontosaurus, and she enthusiastically singles out Hari to me for comment as I am writing my field notes, telling me: 'He is a delight to teach' ... [he is] 'very perky today, gets right into it, even putting rocks in his drawing; he is a delight to teach' (FN, 1/16/97: 9).

My observations suggest that he is indeed 'very perky' that day. He is, for example, an active participant in a Rhyming Bingo activity played by the class near the end of the morning. In this activity, the teacher calls out a word and the children supply a rhyming word to match a picture on their game sheets. Hari at first answers by repeating rhymes supplied by the other children or by providing spontaneous rhymes that do not correspond to those on the Bingo sheet. When he finds that the latter are not acceptable, he soon learns to cue his answers to the game sheet:

Teacher: One that rhymes wi:th ... sto:ne.

Child: [Stone, rone.

Some children: [Stone, bone.

Hari: [Stone, bone.

Teacher: Right, stone, bone.

(*Mrs Clark smiles, looks at me*).

Hari: [I said I said stone, bone.

Children: [(...)

Teacher: [One that rhymes with ...

(Transcript, 1/16/97 and FN 1/16/97: 14)

Mrs Clark smiles and looks at me when he calls out the correct response, seemingly pleased with his progress (FN 1/16/97: 14). When the other children all give the same answer, either on their own or in repetition of Hari, Hari lays claim to the answer as his own and proclaims, 'I said stone, bone.'

Consistent with the teacher's description of him as 'perky,' Hari walks around afterwards, happily singing Bingo repetitively. Soon after that, at dismissal time, he walks around singing a song the children had learned in music class in the fall. As I write my observations of this in my field notes, Mrs Clark approaches me and comments about Hari, using the image of a leader: 'Prime minister ... I think we have a potential leader' (FN 1/16/97: 17).

In an informal conversation after the children have gone, she mentions to me that rhymes are hard for the English language learners and comments that she was 'so pleased that Hari came up to her this morning and told her a rhyme. The first thing he said was "toe/go"' (FN 1/16/97: 17). She tells me that Hari likes rhymes and asks whether I noticed how he was 'into it' when they were playing Rhyming Bingo.

Position

Hari continues to participate actively in the circle activities. In late January, for example, he brings in a battery for sharing, volunteers to say the months of the year, and tells the teacher about a dinosaur 'movie' he saw in computer class (Transcript, 1/23/97). In early February, when Hari is going around getting the other children to sign a birthday card for a classmate, Mrs Clark again approaches me and spontaneously comments about Hari, repeating her characterization of him as a leader: 'We have an organizer here; he takes the leadership, doesn't he?' (FN 2/6/97: 7).

This characterization seems to be prevalent in her mind, for she evokes the image again in mid-February, when she is showing the children their baby pictures (FN 2/18/97: 4). In one picture, Hari is standing waving his arms, and Mrs Clark makes the following comment to him as she shows it around to the class: 'Looks like you, you have people that you're going to make them sing or something. Your arms are waving. Are you pretending to conduct them?' (Transcript, 2/18/97). In another baby picture shown before this one, Hari is sitting on the floor holding a phone.

Teacher: Is he old enough to talk on the phone there?
              (*She shows the picture around to the class. The children are laughing. Hari is laughing: 'Ha, ha, ha, ha, ha, ha, ha, ha.' She takes out another picture from the same envelope*).
Teacher: (He was ...) kind of young to talk on the telephone.
              (*The children continue to laugh; Hari is laughing: 'Ha, ha, ha.'*)

Claudia:	Maybe it's a pretend telephone.
Teacher:	(*laughing*) Ah dear.
Claudia:	Maybe that's a pretend phone. (Transcript, 2/18/97)

Mrs Clark walks around the class showing the picture and engaging in some playful teasing. I may be stretching it to suggest that her playful comments project an image of Hari as capable of talking on the phone. However, Claudia's comments both show that she holds another perspective on Hari and represent a striking resistance to Mrs Clark's interpretation.

In late February, Mrs Clark again makes a comment to me about Hari, who at the time is busily making a character from the Mr Hargreaves story series being read in class: 'He's started to read some Mr Hargreaves books … Hari is quite enjoying. Yesterday he made a … a character from the story' (Transcript, 2/5/97). Her informal comments (and her glances) to me about Hari diminish after this. The only other instances in the data both occur in early April, once when she directs a quick glance at me that I cannot interpret (FN 4/2/97: 3) and another time when she comments after the fact on her reaction to what she interpreted as a nonsense response from Hari when she is asking the children for 'things that do not hatch.'

Jill:	(*calls out*) A rat.
Hari:	How about a shoe hat.
Mrs Clark:	No, we don't think of things like that.
	(*Kids all laugh. Hari in circle looks serious. I can't interpret whether he is serious because he doesn't want teacher to get annoyed or because he thinks his answer is legitimate or other reasons. I see him looking at his shoe and talking to Allan softly. The mike is beside him but I doubt it will pick this up*).
	(*The children go to the tables*). …
Mrs Clark:	(*comments to me*) Did you hear that, the shoe, I just lost control. (*I didn't say much in reply as I was busy writing field notes. I wouldn't interpret teacher's handling of Hari's comment as losing control; she seemed quite polite*). (FN 4/9/97: 6)

It is regrettable that I was not able to query Mrs Clark or Hari about their interpretations of this incident. However, I wonder whether the strong reaction Mrs Clark reported is prompted by the fact that Hari seems to be violating her presumed construction of Hari as a good school child (Walkerdine, 1997).

In order to explore further the import of Mrs Clark's comments, I reviewed and analyzed all the spontaneous interactions between Mrs

Clark and myself recorded in my field notes for the entire year. Besides our social talk and discussion of managerial issues (e.g., scheduling) and classroom incidents, Mrs Clark does occasionally make comments about individual children. She generally expresses pleasure or concern about something specific, and her comment above about Hari's interest in the Mr Men books is a typical example of this. However, in our interactions, Hari is the only one among the children of whom she has spoken in general terms, as for example in her comment 'He is a delight to teach' or given a prognosis for the future: i.e., 'Prime minister ... I think we have a potential leader.'[1]

Hari's position with the teacher (as evidenced in her discourse to me) along with classroom practices, in which she scaffolds and encourages his speech and participation in circles, offer Hari a safe and comfortable position from which to speak.[2] Hari maintains active participation in the circle activities throughout the rest of the year. He often replies, sometimes lengthily, to Mrs Clark's questions, contributes to sharing and circle talk, guesses at guessing bag time, and volunteers to read the reading message.

A particularly striking example of Hari's participation occurred in an observation in early March, when the two kindergarten classes in the school were combined to listen to a presentation by a visiting Block Parent. When the Parent asks a question, Hari bids persistently, and when called on, makes two contributions, the second of which is particularly lengthy.

Hari: If you get hurt and we can go home, tell our parent our friend is hurt and call to hospital.

Parent: Tell the parent and they decide whether to call the hospital.
...
Parent: When are times you would go to a block parent?
              (*Hari's hand goes up like a shot. He gets called on and gives a long answer*).

Hari: If some cars coming, the boy is walking on the road and he's fall down and ... and ... then we have to go and knock on the door and tell my friend just died.

Parent: (*a bit surprised*)   Well, we hope he wouldn't die.... (FN 3/4/97: 8–9)

The mid-year teacher interview happened to be scheduled on the same day as the above observation was made:

Elaine: Now so with Hari, he pretty much interacts with most children, you were saying?

Mrs Clark: I think so, yes. And he ... is forever putting his hand up and saying, has things to contribute in our discussions. For example, today that, that visitor we had with the Block Parents in his long story about what would happen if the car came along and the tire went over the friend and ... another time about somebody would get hurt and go to the hospital and (*laughs a bit*) you know, he's quite (*pause*)

Elaine: He's quite imaginative.

Mrs Clark: But this is it, but he's also got the confidence that with the two classrooms of kindergarten children in here, 40 children, that he has the confidence in his English-speaking abilities to put his hand up to that stranger and make a big long comment like that. I think that takes gumption, you know. (Teacher interview, 3/4/97)

As one can see from the transcript, Mrs Clark comments favorably on Hari's classroom participation, using his reply to the Block Parent as an example. Perhaps remembering the vividness of his response, I interpret Hari's contribution as imaginative, whereas Mrs Clark names emotional/affective factors as significant. Recalling his behavior in the early months of the school year, she continues:

Mrs Clark: ... I don't think we would have seen that in September or October.

Elaine: No I'm trying to think back.

...

Mrs Clark: I, I seem to recall him as being a fairly timid, reserved child in the beginning, but he's come way, way out of that now.

A final example in June suggests how questions of access are interrelated with Hari's confidence and eagerness to participate. In this example, Mrs Clark is reading a book on bees, and when she explains that nectar turns into honey, she asks the children if they eat honey. Hari raises his hand, calls out 'Mrs Clark,' and keeps his hand up waiting to be called on. Kevin raises his hand, and noticing this, Hari raises his hand higher. The two boys then 'engage in a hand-raising match, holding their arms high, and putting them one against the other' (FN 6/9/97: 5). Mrs Clark notices this, hesitates on whom to call, and decides on another child, Eva, instead. After Eva replies, she calls on Hari, who volunteers a lengthy narrative, and then calls on Kevin, who offers a brief contribution, which from my perspective seems more relevant to the discussion than does Hari's narrative.

Hari: Um I, I was ... and I watch it and they was talking about the honey, the honey bee (*a few children say honey bee with him*), and then it did it did went went to the honey bee tree, and all the, all the honey bee, it, it, it, all the honey bee were, they get out, and then they they get in the bus and the bus is magic, and and he get in the magic, magic school bus bus, he (say) to a honey bee and then they got the honey bees out of, they were in.

Teacher: Wow, so that was interesting, the magic school bus went right to the honey, to the hive? the bee hive? I don't know that story.

...

Teacher: ... Yes, Kevin.
Kevin: Um the bees (usually) come to suck um the the
Teacher: Nectar?
Kevin: Yes. (Transcript, 6/9/97)

Identification

The previous examples suggest that Hari had a special position in Mrs Clark's eyes, a situation which may have given him a place and contributed to his confidence and willingness to participate in whole-class activities. Hari readily appropriates interaction time with Mrs Clark and is quite confident in doing so. However, he remains more ambiguous in this respect when with classmates (see Chapter 5). Hari also tries to maintain and enhance the position that Mrs Clark has offered him, as we will now see.

In January, Hari begins to initiate a kind of spontaneous comment to Mrs Clark that I did not observe in the first three months of school; the nature of these comments is to reinforce or add to what she is trying to teach. The following incident occurs just after the children had done the days of the week and month routines. Hari calls out in the slight pause before the start of the numbers routine.

Hari: [Miss Clark, Miss Clark.
Teacher: [Our number line
Hari: Miss Clark
Teacher: How many days have we been at school now?
Child: Eighty-one
Children: Eigh:ty-one
Child: Eighty-one
Hari: We going closer (*'closer' pronounced as 'clozer'*).
Child: Eighteen zero, eighteen zero.

Teacher: Eighty-one, how do I make an eighty-one?

...

Hari: Miss Clark, Miss Clark, we going closer to one hundred (*'closer' pronounced as 'clozer'*).

Teacher: We are getting closer to one hundred.

...

Hari: Miss Clark ... (Transcript, 1/16/97)

(*He gets up, goes over to the calendar, points and says, 'This is gonna be this number.' Mrs Clark glances at me, nudging her jaw down slightly, kind of like a slight 'I'm impressed' look*). (FN 1/16/97: 12)

In this incident, Hari calls out to the teacher and makes an independent observation about the progress of the class on the number line. When Mrs Clark continues with the lesson, he persists and repeats his observation, receiving an acknowledgment. He then addresses her again. My field notes indicate that Hari then physically moves to the front of the room and shows the teacher the number, an initiative that engenders an approving glance from Mrs Clark to me.

And in the afternoon, when the teacher asks the children what they know about a brontosaurus, I record the following interactions:

Teacher: (*re brontosaurus*) He eats rocks!

Child: No:

Teacher: Yes, he eats rocks, Hari's right. Why does he eat rocks?

Hari: Because he, if the plant and the tree mix up.

Teacher: That's right. He doesn't have a kind of teeth to chew up his leaves and his plants that he eats. He just swallows them without chewing them up ... to eat rocks because the rocks in his tummy, and the rocks mix around with all those leaves and plants and mush up his food, mush up the leaves and things. So he does eat rocks. That helps him to digest his food. That's very good. Baldev, what else can you tell us? (Transcript, 1/16/97)

(*I hear Hari mumbling 'right'*). (FN 1/16/97: 4)

When Hari volunteers a reply to the teacher's question and she expands on his answer, Hari confirms her expansion, saying 'right.' In this way, he keeps control of his response and maintains equivalence with her.

Field notes of subsequent observations reveal many examples throughout the year of the ways in which Hari plays an active role in identifying with the teacher and taking on her role. For example, he reinforces classroom rules, as is shown in the following example in which Mrs Clark has just announced that it is recess time:

> (*Hari moves toward the teacher, as the children get up to get their coats*).

Hari: Miss Clark, Miss Clark (…) and when we have to when we go outside and when (…) we (…) on the swings (…) 'cause it's not, it didn't, then we (…)

Mrs Clark: You'll remember the rules, that's right. (Transcript, 3/12/97)

Hari also tries to anticipate the teacher. For example, as Mrs Clark walks over to the May calendar in front of the room, he calls out 'Thomas, Thomas' and she then says, 'It is six days to Thomas' birthday' (FN 5/26/97: 3).

He also echoes the teacher's instructional discourse, as in the following recording when the teacher is preparing the children to make a lantern for Chinese New Year.

Nadia: I make it for (…) Grade 1.

Teacher: You (made it) when you were in the Grade 1 class, did you? All right, and what do we have …

Child: Lantern.

> (*Teacher talks about lantern; Hari twice calls 'Miss Clark' but she continues*).

Hari: Miss Clark, Miss Clark, don't you know, I, when I go to school (…)

Hari: And then we make that.

Teacher: Did you?

Hari: Yea: and and we cut off the lines. We, we painted in the lines, red, different lines, and we cut out, and we (…) and we had to do it, and when we do it (…), one (fit) on the other and went down and one (handle) ended and (it) then you have to, you have this one piece of paper and the other one (this way) and put it, put it in it and then we have to pull off the (…) and then up, we have to put eyes.

Teacher: Oh, sounds fancy.

Hari: And put our name on it and we have to put it in (…) Christmas tree.

Teacher: Oh it was for a Christmas tree …

Hari: And and we (…) all the decorations.

Teacher: Wow, fancy. All right, so now … (Transcript, 2/6/97)

Hari gives a long step-by-step explanation of how they made a lantern in his pre-school – an uncanny echo of the kinds of directions she gives them for doing their craft activities. His readiness to provide this explanation is in contrast to Nadia at the beginning, who has simply commented that she made one in her Grade 1 class (this girl had been switched from Grade 1 to kindergarten).

As in the previous example about the number line, Hari externalizes his thinking and spontaneously adds information to the teacher's lesson in another instance, when the children are printing the letter 'k' on their kites: 'Mrs Clark, k, k for kite, k for Mrs Clark! ' (Transcript, 3/4/97). In a further example, recorded both in my field notes and on video, Mrs Clark is asking what the baby cow is called, as she refers to the poster of a cow on the easel.

Some
children: Calf.
Teacher: They're the babies, they're the calves. (*Reads the sentence at the bottom of the easel, pointing to each word*) 'Calf, a baby cow is a calf.' (*Walks back toward her chair, saying:*)
[The mother is the cow, the baby is the calf.
Hari: [Er, er, er, and, and the black and white look like the polar.
Teacher: (*looking at poster*) Mhmhm, he's black and white, or dark brown and white, (*looking at Hari*) same coloring isn't he as a polar bear; (*looking at children*) but cows and calves come in all kinds of colors, different colors.
Thomas: I saw one. (Video transcript, 5/12/97)

Hari offers an independent observation as the teacher goes to sit down, and the teacher accepts this, pausing to look at the poster, and expanding on what he says.

In addition, Hari becomes increasingly industrious at the craft and work activities as the year goes by, reflecting the teacher's emphasis on hard work and colorful drawings. In the following example from May (5/12/97), the children are making cows out of paper towel rolls; Mrs Clark is circulating around the room. My notes indicate that Hari is making a very colorful cow, using about six colors, in contrast to Sue's and Jason's cows, which are in one color, and Casey's, which is in two (FN 5/12/97: 6).

Hari: I making colorful things.
Teacher: You like to do all these colorful things these days. Why is that, Hari? (…) 'cause Victor does colorful things? (…) You just like colorful things? … (Transcript, 5/12/97)

When Mrs Clark is in the area, Hari calls his colorful work to her attention.

She accepts his comment and makes the suggestion that he may be modeling himself on another child in the afternoon class (whom she considers to be an excellent artist), but Hari rejects her suggestion. Later at the same table, as the children continue their work, I hear Hari comment, 'I like coloring. I like a hard work' (Transcript, 5/12/97).

In our final observation in mid-June, the class has to fill in a survey which the teacher tells me is for the school's accreditation. The children have to fill in boxes indicating 'yes,' 'no,' or 'maybe' to each of the questions read out by the teacher. They check their boxes with gusto and happily call out their responses to themselves and those around them.

Teacher: … All right, number 8 says (*pause*)
Hari: (*whispering*) Yea, yea, yea.
Teacher: I am learning about music.
Hari: Music, yes.
…

                (*Later*)
Teacher: Are we listening? I am good at thinking of new ideas.
**Some
children:**   Yes.
Hari: Yes, I think new [ideas.
Teacher: [Yes, no, or you're not sure beside number 13.
Hari: I say yes, yes, yes, 1, 2, 3, 4, 5, 6, 7, 8, 9, 10, 11, 12, 13, 14.
Child: …
Child: I don't know.
Hari: (*to teacher*) I did one.
Teacher: Thirteen, I am good at thinking of new ideas. Rajinder, yes, no, not sure, you fill in one of those.
Hari: I got 13 already. 1, 2, 3, 4, 5, 6, 7, all (…) (Transcript, 6/17/97)

Hari fills out the survey enthusiastically, answering 'yes' to every question. The above excerpt is typical of those found in the transcript for that activity and shows him being the good pedagogic pupil that his teacher desires him to be.

In the teacher interview conducted in June, Mrs Clark describes Hari's progress in very positive terms, setting him above the other children in the sample: 'has shown the most growth of everybody … he's really amazing …' (Teacher interview, 6/9/97). She provides detailed evidence of Hari's abilities in the ensuing conversation (good listening skills, very good at rhymes, makes logical guesses at guessing bag, knows personal information, can count to 100, etc.). The one area where Hari 'needs work,' in her judgment, is his last name: 'He still doesn't get his last name.' Mrs Clark attributes Hari's progress to his parents' interest in his school work and their desire for him to do well:

Mrs Clark: I think he's really quite a smart little guy. And you know, what do I attribute that to? Well, his mom and dad are very interested. His mom is always, forever checking with me to see how he's doing, which is a lot more than some of the other parents do. They are anxious for him to do well. And whether they've just got a different outlook on education from the home, I don't know. But he really, he really is showing great growth, I think.... (Teacher interview, 6/9/97)

Near the end of the interview, she mentions that Hari doesn't ever want to be wrong and characterizes him as law-abiding, acknowledging that this may be why she likes him:

Mrs Clark: He doesn't want to ever be wrong. He is quite disturbed that his name is on the board right now because he's forgotten his library book.... He didn't like that.... He again has a very clear idea of what's right and what's wrong. And he is very law-abiding. I really, I think he's a law-abiding student, which maybe is why I quite like him. (Teacher interview, 6/9/97)

Her final words recounting to me an incident in which Hari put a crayon in place in the classroom are telling:

Mrs Clark: It was funny now this morning we all lined up to go up to music.... He was toward the end of the line. He looked back at the classroom. When he saw that purple container of fat crayons on the table, he stepped out of line and came back and brought it, put it right, rightful spot. He's just you know, I find that quite, quite a mature thing for a five-year-old ... quite touching.

The fusion of responsibility and affectivity are crystallized in the words chosen to characterize his action: 'quite touching.' The child who crept into her heart at the beginning of the year is also the child who assumes responsibility for the minute details of her class at the end.

Discussion

Following Vygotsky, contemporary sociocultural theorists look for shifts or changes in participation as indicative of development. They stress that when these happen, change occurs both in the learner and in the inter-personal relationships between learner and expert (Lave & Wenger, 1991; Miller & Goodnow, 1995). In this chapter, I showed how Hari dramatically increased his participation in the classroom over the year and traced how his relationship with his teacher also changed. I also probed into some of the underlying reasons for these changes, using critical psychoanalytic theories on the interconnections between power relations and unconscious desires to guide my interpretation.

The critical psychologist Litowitz (1993) argues that we need to have a greater understanding of motivational and affective issues in learning and that this requires a more complex conceptualization of subjectivity, which includes the dimension of the unconscious. Litowitz introduces the psychoanalytic construct of identification to help understand why we learn. She bases her analysis on Lacan, for whom desire is assumed to be the motivating principle of human life, and the 'other' is the position of control of desire and meaning. And she hypothesizes that the desire to be the adult or to be the one whom the adult wants him to be is what motivates a child to master a task.

Litowitz (1997) quotes Vygotsky's maxim that all development consists in the fact that the development of a function goes from me to 'I' (p. 481).[3] She writes of this shift in the following way:

> The desire to move beyond participation to responsibility is in itself an act of resistance, a resistance to being dependent and controlled by another. The motivation cannot be mastery of the other's skill but to be the other *by means of* mastery of the skill. (p. 482)

For Litowitz then, the process of identification is one which also engenders resistance, and we do this by taking on the other's role.

Litowitz writes that it is important to reexamine not only 'what we are asking the learner to do but whom we are asking the learner to be' in educational settings (Litowitz, 1997: 479). Goodnow (1990a) hypothesizes: 'The negotiations one is willing to work on are likely to be those with people one perceives as similar, wishes to be like, or wishes to impress' (p. 283).

These two researchers criticize current work in sociocultural theory as 'too exclusively concerned with what is being done by the dispensers of knowledge' (p. 280) and not concerned enough with what the child's perspective might be. Litowitz (1993, 1997) suggests that it might be productive to see the child as learning in what Winnicott (1971) calls a 'holding environment' or 'potential space,' where illusion and fantasy play an important role in addition to play and imagination, as hypothesized by Vygotsky. Following Winnicott, Litowitz (1993) explains this as: 'the range of the child's grandiosity and omnipotence. In that space the child sees herself as more capable than she really is' (p. 190).

Litowitz (1997) theorizes that as young children learn their first language, they have 'a grandiose fantasy of enhanced performance' that allows them to speak, even though their mastery is far from that of adults: 'By speaking, children feel like adults and hear themselves as more competent speakers.' She questions the adult's role in this, suggesting that the adult similarly has a fantasy 'that the child can be/is becoming just like her/him' (p. 478).

Litowitz is writing about first language learning in children and about the parent–child relationship, and one must be wary of extrapolating to children learning a second language and the teacher–child relationship. However, it is striking how resonant the theoretical perspectives she proposes are with the data.

This chapter demonstrates how Mrs Clark may have played a role in fostering a 'grandiose fantasy of enhanced performance' through practices in which she scaffolds and encourages Hari's speech and participation in circles. Stone (1993) specifies one of the communicative mechanisms involved in scaffolding as 'prolepsis,' a term which 'refers to a communicative move in which the speaker presupposes some as yet unprovided information' (p. 171). Mrs Clark's questions in the excerpt about Power Rangers and Halloween seem to be an example of this.

We also saw how the teacher viewed Hari for a certain period of the year, visibly signaling to me her pleasure with and approval of some of his verbal contributions and projecting an image of him as a leader, in other words perhaps as someone like herself. In fact, her projection of Hari as a future leadership type could be seen as another kind of prolepsis.

I suggested that these supportive behaviors by Mrs Clark might be among the reasons that Hari maintains a strong participation in circle activities throughout the year, showing as Mrs Clark said, unusual self-confidence for an English language learner. Hari finds a place to have a voice and attempts to take on the teacher's role by ventriloquating rules and instructions, anticipating the teacher, and displaying and adding to classroom learning.

Following Litowitz (1997), who argues that identification is bi-directional, I suggest that a mutual process of identification arose between Hari and the teacher, with the teacher projecting her own image onto Hari and Hari responding to this. Who followed and who led in this is not important; for whatever reason, this process created a 'potential space' or 'holding environment' (in Winnicott's sense), in which Hari's further development could take place. In this space, Hari can take on a powerful position and display mastery and control of highly valued classroom knowledge and skills (e.g., rhymes, colorful drawings, knowing the rules).

Miller and Goodnow (1995) identify the formation of emotional bonds between people as one of the many affective consequences of participating in everyday discourse. They suggest that we should consider practices not only in terms of identity but also in terms of emotional investment:

> Because practices recur in everyday life, they provide participants with repeated opportunities to invest in values, in ways of interpreting experience, and in the practice itself. Here, too, participation leaves its mark on the person through the production of affective stance: enthusiastic involvement, indifference, resistance, playfulness. And, like ability and identity, affective stance is likely to get created and re-created in practice. (p. 14)

Following Foucault, critical and poststructural theorists (e.g., Henriques *et al.*, 1984; Walkerdine, 1997; Weedon, 1987) argue more emphatically that when we take on social positions, we also take on the psychic and emotional structure implicit in them. As Weedon (1987) explains, 'discourses ... constitute the meaning of the physical body, psychic energy, the emotions and desire, as well as conscious subjectivity.... They define individual identities and the forms of pleasure derived from them' (p. 112).

With respect to the second language research, researchers working on identity in second language learning have concentrated mainly on learners; consequently, they have perhaps not given quite enough attention to the mutuality of relationships between learners and the others with whom they are involved. Norton's work (Norton, 2000), for example, relies on diary studies and accounts by adult learners of their experiences. McKay and Wong's study (1996) in secondary school considers observational data of classroom interactions and teacher interview data, but their analysis of teacher discourse is done in terms of broad categories and thus perhaps limits a fuller consideration of the others. Bell's work (1995, 1997a) suggestively explores the importance of examining relationships between teachers and learners, especially, as in Bell's case, where the researcher is also the learner. As well, the data I have discussed illustrate the need to keep firmly in view the 'relational patterning' (Urwin, 1984: 290) between the learner and those with whom she is involved.

In her study of the Cohort 1 kindergarten children in this project, Toohey (2000) shows the dynamic processes involved in how school identities are constructed and how children take up these identities. Canagarajah (1993) also discusses dynamism and contradictions in how students respond to power relations inherent in these processes. He argues that we should pay more attention to 'the issue of how domination reaches into the structure of the personality itself' (p. 603). In her study of identity in secondary students in South Africa, Thesen (1997) argues that it is important to go beyond a deterministic view of identity. She advocates a Bakhtinian perspective so that we pay greater attention to the voices of individual learners.

Though all of these lines of research are productive, the issues are complex. For further understanding we should also look to psychoanalytic theories, which put issues such as motivation, desire, power, and control at the center of our attention. This approach falls in line with Bourne's (1992) argument that we need to recognize that there are unconscious and powerful drives at work in how we take up social positions. As this chapter suggests, these drives are at work not only in how we take up these positions but also in the positioning that we offer to others.

Summary

I showed how power relations and unconscious emotional or affective factors seemed to be operating in the child–teacher relationship, and I proposed that a mutual process of identification arose between Hari and the teacher, with the teacher projecting her own image of him onto Hari and Hari responding to this by maintaining and enhancing the position she offered. In this relationship, Hari actively displayed his competence, created many opportunities for practice, and was very confident in doing so. To close, I stressed the importance of viewing learning as relational and suggested the need to incorporate psychoanalytic understandings into the current framework on identity and second language learning.

Notes

1. In the formal interviews conducted three times during the year, Mrs Clark makes general comments about the sample children but there are no future prognoses either about Hari or the others.
2. It is important to note that sociocultural theorists consider not only verbal but nonverbal communicative devices, such as gestures, eye gazes, and pauses, to be important components of the scaffolding process (Rogoff *et al.*, 1993; Stone, 1993).
3. Litowitz cites this quotation as a concrete reflection of her argument that pronoun acquisition in children involves not only learning linguistic forms and rules but also learning social relations. She proposes that when children learn to refer to themselves as 'I' instead of using 'me' (or their personal name), this represents a critical shift in which they also learn that they can take on the position of subject ('I') as opposed to object for another ('me'). For Litowitz, pronouns signal social relations and self-identification, and learning to use them involves not merely learning linguistic forms and rules but also learning to participate reciprocally and then reversibly in discourses with others.

Chapter 8
Conclusions

In this work, I followed the learning trajectory of a Punjabi-speaking English language learner in kindergarten in the context of his relations with his classmates and teacher. The theoretical perspectives I drew from include Bakhtin's (1981, 1984a,b, 1986) and Vygotsky's (1978, 1986) theories on language and learning, the work of contemporary sociocultural theorists on situated learning (Lave & Wenger, 1991), and poststructural theories on identity (Henriques *et al.*, 1984; Weedon, 1987). In this framework, language learning is viewed as a socioculturally situated social practice that engages learners' social identities; from this perspective, questions of access to and participation in various forms of learning activities are critical. Guided by these theories, I was able to respond to calls for research on the social and subjective dimensions of language learning – areas which until recently have been on the margins of the field (McGroarty, 1998).

Summary

I focused on the kindergarten 'career' of one English language learner, Hari. Examining his experiences, I showed the complexity and variability of peer relations in this kindergarten classroom and the critical role they played in the identities learners could negotiate and the kinds of access and participation they could have. In some situations Hari was positioned as not strong and as lower in status, particularly by the more powerful boys in his class. Hari had strategies for resisting the positions he was offered, but these were not always effective. In the expanded view of competence proposed by Bourdieu (1977), Hari clearly did not have the 'the power to impose reception' with some of his classmates and this did not change with time despite his growing fluency in English.

In his relationship with Casey, a newcomer to the class in late January, Hari had a respected place; over time, their relationship underwent a qualitative shift, such that one could speak of the development of a friendship between the two boys. Their activity time play showed how Hari was able to negotiate identity and linguistic and other resources on an ongoing basis in a relationship of caring, trust, and reciprocity. Hari was able to appropriate the English language freely and take on a voice, a place from which to speak, under conditions which did not threaten or constrain him. These conditions were obtained with Casey and also with his teacher, Mrs Clark.

I showed how Hari had a valued place with his teacher and how he transformed his participation and played an active role in maintaining and enhancing the position she offered. In addition, I showed how power relations and unconscious emotional or affective factors seemed to be operating in the child–teacher relationship and proposed that a mutual process of identification arose between Hari and the teacher, with the teacher projecting her own image onto Hari and Hari responding to this. In this relationship, Hari actively displayed his competence, created many opportunities for practice, and was very confident in doing so. Of particular interest was the fact that he chose to tell stories about himself in the circle, where he perhaps found safety and an audience that were not always available elsewhere.

Overall, I showed that Hari had different social value with different members of his class and that these evaluations influenced the identities he displayed, his access, his participation, and his opportunities for learning.

Discussion

Lave and Wenger's (1991) theory of learning as legitimate peripheral participation in a community of practice provided a framework with which I was able to trace Hari's opportunities for learning in his classroom. This theory allowed me to see Hari as a learner involved in many sub-communities in his class and able to take on diverse roles within them. Their emphasis on analyzing the development of these communities over time and their political and social organization helped me understand the complexity of power relations and how these affected Hari's access to practice.

Bakhtinian and contemporary poststructural theories on the political and complex nature of our everyday interactions shed light on the complex positioning and counter-positioning of the children and provided a window on the intricacy of their social relations. The emphasis on discourse shifts as a way of seeking points of assertion illuminated how Hari managed to actively position himself in the interactions.

Bourdieu's (1977, 1991) theories on the importance of symbolic power relations among speakers enriched my understanding of some of the constraints Hari experienced in these interactions. Bakhtin's (1986) insistence on our potential for symbolic freedom through language served well in helping me understand Hari's ability to overcome, at least partially, some of the obstacles he encountered. I recall how he seized on openings in the more open spaces of the classroom to display a more powerful identity and how he escaped a difficult situation through language play. I also note how Hari skillfully used syllable segmentation, a practice highly valued in the classroom, in some of these interactions. Although sometime unsuccessful, his improvizations nevertheless showed how Hari made use of his second language (English) as a powerful resource for claiming a voice, a place from which to speak.

I briefly described how Hari's language grew over the year, focusing mainly on his verb usage and noting the considerable variability I observed. Although variability is a controversial issue for SLA researchers (Ellis, 1994), it is consistent with the view of language as dynamic and situated speech activity. Bakhtin's view of language as a powerful resource for claiming a voice and his emphasis on the sociopolitical conditions of speaking provided a valuable lens for understanding this variability.

I presented a view of the language learner as socially embedded, drawing in particular on Norton's (2000) conceptualization of identity as multiple and complex, dynamic and a site of struggle. I also discussed some of the problems encountered in overcoming dualistic conceptualizations of the person as a unitary monad divorced from social context. In examining the child–teacher relationship, I found that a social construction analysis (showing how subjects are produced through social practices) was useful for accounting for some of the data. However, it could not account for other data I was finding on how Hari took up his positioning, and I had to look to other theoretical perspectives to understand these. The work of Litowitz (1997) introduced me to psychoanalytic perspectives on learning and opened up a way to see how Hari was actively constructing his position with the teacher. I pursued this line of thought through further reading, drawing particularly on the work of scholars who combine selected aspects of psychoanalytic theory with critical theoretical perspectives (Henriques *et al.*, 1984; Walkerdine, 1997). These psychoanaltytic theories about learning allowed me to explore the role of identification and unconscious desires in learning – important areas that have been little investigated in the second language field (Ibrahim, 1999).[1] They also enabled me to expand the conceptualization of the person proposed by Norton (2000).

Finally, but no less important, ethnography proved valuable with its requirements of prolonged engagement, painstaking attention to the detailed specifics of classroom life, and interpretive understanding.

Implications for Research

As many researchers have noted (e.g., Davis, 1995; Firth & Wagner, 1997;

Lazaraton, 1995; Rampton, 1991), much research on second language learning has been undertaken from a cognitive perspective, seeing learning as individual acquisition of language viewed as a body of knowledge. Researchers have considered social and contextual factors but have treated these as variables influencing individual functioning. Recent years have seen an increase in ethnographic studies which situate learners in their sociocultural context. And critical researchers have made important contributions showing how power relations and social context cannot be divorced from considerations of learning (e.g., Cummins, 1996, 2000; Norton, 2000; Toohey, 2000).

In the 1990s, some researchers have used both critical/poststructural and sociocultural/historical perspectives in conducting ethnographic research on the social, cultural, and political dimensions of second language learning (e.g., Blackledge, 2000; Canagarajah, 1993; Gutierrez & Larson, 1994; Hall, 1998; Norton, 2000; Toohey, 2000; Vasquez et al., 1994). The community of people working in these joint perspectives, though increasing, is still small; however, their work is suggestive and points to a promising direction for second language research.

I examined the experiences of one child in his relationship with others, using these combined theoretical perspectives in conjunction with critical psychoanalytic theories (e.g., Henriques et al., 1984). The empirical data I presented suggest the helpfulness of such analyses in developing more complex understandings of the learner–teacher relationship, the need for which many second language researchers have expressed (e.g., Firth & Wagner, 1997; Norton & Toohey, 2001; Rampton, 1991, 1995). For this reason, I suggest that research undertaken from a broader framework, which includes a critical psychoanalytic perspective, may provide another useful area of exploration in addition to the productive avenues suggested by previous second language work on identity. This broader framework explores how emotional commitments and affectivity interconnect with power relations; it emphasizes the complexity of human relationships and deals with how actual subjectivities are constructed in everyday practices.

One thread running through the last two chapters of this book is the phenomenon of prolepsis, which Cole (1996) has defined as 'the representation of a future act or development as being presently existing' (p. 183). In Chapter 6, we saw how Casey imagined future possibilities for Hari and projected an image of Hari as master or expert. We also saw how the two boys built an imaginary world through play, which itself is proleptic, and how Hari had a valued identity there.

In Chapter 7, prolepsis was manifested in some of the teacher's scaffolding practices, and in a broader sense, in the teacher's projection of

Hari's future. It was also seen in the hypothesized 'holding environment' she provided, where Hari could imagine his place and take on a voice. In this place, Hari took on the teacher's role and a powerful place from which to speak.

All of these situations seemed to me to suggest that it will be important to explore the role of imagination in second language education. Such research can range from investigation into the semiotics of scaffolding and other devices which help establish a shared perspective (as in some current work, e.g., Antón & DiCamilla, 1998) to exploration of broader areas of human activity. Wenger proposes that the imagination is a distinct way of belonging, referring to the imagination as 'a process of expanding our self by transcending our time and space and creating new images of the world and ourselves' (Wenger, 1998: 176). Norton (2001) shows how the realm of learners' communities extends to the imagined world outside the classroom and how learners' desires to preserve the integrity of their 'imagined communities' enters into the extent to which they invest in the second language. For me, when we learn a second language, we need to creatively imagine ourselves in another community. Perhaps Casey and Hari's teacher offered Hari a way, a place for imagined possibilities to become a reality.

Implications for Classrooms

In examining Hari's relationship with his teacher, I showed the powerful role of the teacher in teacher–child relationships, where power is seen as 'a network of relations constantly in tension and ever-present in activity' rather than as something which is possessed (Corson, 1993: 4). In the relationship I examined, the teacher gave the child a place in the interactions and held it for him; she gave him a voice that could speak from a desirable and powerful identity. The child gained social capital in the classroom.

I have not analyzed data with respect to the children who spoke from different places, but I can speculate that had the opposite been the case, Hari's participation and progress might not have increased, as for example with some of the children (e.g., Surjeet and Harvey) in Toohey's study (Toohey, 2000). However, I would caution that this is one particular case, depending on local understandings. The issues are very complicated, as shown, for example, by Willett (1995) in her study of four English language learners in Grade 1 and by Hunter (1997) in her study of an English language learner in Grades 4 and 5.

I hope my work will encourage teachers to recognize how power relations operate in their interactions with learners and to take measures that enhance sharing power with students. In this regard, work on enhancing collaborative talk structures in classrooms (e.g., Guttierez & Larson, 1994; Gutierrez *et al.*, 1995; Pappas, 1999) is of crucial importance. I also note how important opportunities for oral storytelling were for Hari in helping him gain a sense of belonging in the classroom and point to Dyson and Genishi's (1994) work in incorporating this genre more fully in the classroom. In addition, teachers need to carefully reflect on their power, including examining their own feelings through personal reflection, diary and journal writing, and collegial discussion.

Building interpersonal bonds and fostering a sense of community in classrooms should be a prime consideration for teachers. Collaborative learning arrangements, peer tutoring and buddy systems, are all potentially helpful, as well as genres of talk such as word play, storytelling, interpersonal repartee and song (e.g., Hall & Verplaetse, 2000). However, I have shown some of the intricacy of children's social relations and the need to give far greater consideration to issues of power and status than has been the case in past.

Teachers need to put human relationships at the center of learning and consider both affective and political dimensions of classroom life as central and not peripheral. Some of the data in this study show the importance of having friends in school. In her study of multilingual classrooms in Great Britain, Bourne (1992, quoting Davies) emphasizes the value of friendship in maneuvering the world of school:

> To be alone in a new place without friends is potentially devastating. To find a friend is to partially alleviate the problem. By building with that friend a system of shared meanings and understanding, such that the world is a predictable place, children take the first step towards being competent people within the social setting of the school. (Davies, 1982, cited in Bourne, 1992: 443–444)

As teachers know, one has to walk a fine line between allowing children to be near friends in classroom seating and activities and having children work with a variety of others. However, it is still important to recognize how important friendship can be, so that teachers may tread gently when they move children away from their friends or disrupt a friendship.

Some of the data in this study are quite suggestive of the work described by other researchers (Kanno, 2000; Kanno & Applebaum, 1995; McKay & Wong, 1996; Miller, 1999, 2000), in which some English language learners describe difficulties in establishing social relationships with their classmates. Teachers need to develop structures that facilitate social relations in classrooms and help us counter some of the positioning practices I observed. For example, Paley (1992), a classroom teacher, researcher, and author, challenges our accepted ways of thinking about play as a private domain and tries to develop classroom structures that break down hierarchies and overcome exclusion and rejection. Her work provides a model of how to engage with students in effecting this kind of change in classrooms and schools. Of particular interest are her use of story as a way of framing discussions with children and her willingness to negotiate and develop classroom structures with them. Making children aware of the power of their interactions to create their world, and giving them the opportunity to articulate their feelings, listen to one another, and be involved in creating an environment that helps to treat one another with empathy and respect are critical ingredients in this work. Paley warns that effecting change of this nature is very difficult and requires ongoing work with every group of students she teaches.

In addition, I hope this study will bring awareness of children's ongoing positionings and counter-positionings. As Hari's case shows, sometimes children are effective in their strategies of resistance, and sometimes they are not. Remembering that they are not is important, and thinking of ways to assist students in this area might be useful. However, even more important is Paley's (1992) suggestion that we try to change our own attitudes and expectations rather than try to change the outsider to be more acceptable to the insider.

Changing the outsider to be more acceptable to the insider occurs in many ways in classrooms and schools. The things to be changed often include outside-school characteristics, such as home languages and cultures. Bourdieu (1991) argues that schools reinforce the knowledge and values of the dominant group (s) and that students unconsciously learn and accept these as the norm ('symbolic domination'). For example, Hari learned the relative status of his two languages and was coming to accept the dominant language, English, as the norm. A rich body of literature on bilingual and multicultural education (e.g., Cummins, 1996, 2000; Faltis & Hudelson, 1998; Nieto, 1999; Vasquez *et al.*, 1994) makes clear that teachers, classrooms and schools can successfully change their attitudes and expectations toward children of diverse language backgrounds and intentionally build on the rich linguistic and cultural experiences they bring to school. Openly valuing the local language (s), learning them, incorporating home language practices into classroom activities, establishing links between the home and school, and inviting community members into the classroom, are among the many measures that have been shown to be effective (e.g., Blackledge, 2000; Cummins, 1996, 2000; Nieto, 1999; Vasquez *et al.*, 1994).

In all areas, ethnographic work by teachers in their classrooms, other forms of teacher inquiry, and structures to support these are important for enhancing our understanding (Bell, 1997b; Wells, 1994; Wells & Chang-Wells, 1992). The concept 'teacher research' encompasses multiple meanings and involves controversial issues related to voice, power and status (McCarty, 1997; Richardson, 1994). Finding ways for teachers and university researchers to engage in respectful discussion and dialogue will be critical (Coulter, 1999; Toohey, 2000; Toohey & Waterstone, 2001). This text is offered as one university-based researcher's contribution to that dialogue.

A promising initiative and possible model lies in the Simon Fraser University Teacher Action Research Group, made up of teachers and university-based researchers, who have met weekly over the last two years to reflect on teaching practices in ethnically diverse, multilingual classrooms and collaborate on ethnographic projects therein. Accounts of their ethnographic projects, dialogues, reflections, and critiques can be found in the following works: Denos, in press; Denos *et al.*, 2001; Denos *et al.*, in press; Waterstone, 2001. Another model can be found in Pappas and Zecker's (2001) account of a school–university project in which teachers struggled to establish collaborative power structures in the ethnically and linguistically diverse classrooms in which they taught.

Limitations of the Study

It is important to remember that this account represents my interpretations of classroom events and privileges my voice as researcher. It does not represent fully the teacher's interpretations of classroom events, nor Hari's, nor his parents', nor his classmates'. This research, although conducted in the ethnographic tradition, has pointed out strongly to me the problematics associated with observation and analysis of other people's interactions and behaviors. In future research, I hope to take more fully into account insiders' interpretations as I create my representations. At the same time, I am mindful that the problem of perspectival seeing always remains in any piece of research (Bordo, 1990; Van Maanen, 1995).

In this study, I primarily examined the interactions of one child. The complexity of these interactions and of the classroom relationships were sufficiently daunting that I feel I have examined them only in a surface sense. While the emphasis on one child alone may be seen as a limitation of the work, I hope that this focused examination has permitted me to uncover some of the richness and intricacy of the classroom I observed.

Final Comments

In this study, I conducted a detailed analysis of the social relationships of Hari, a Punjabi-speaking English language learner, in his first year of school and showed the critical role those relationships played in the identities he could negotiate and the kinds of access, participation, and opportunities for language learning he could have. In addition, I showed how power relations and unconscious emotional or affective factors were at work in Hari's relationship with his teacher and suggested the concept of the unconscious as an important consideration for future work on identity and second language learning. I also suggested that it will be important to explore the role of imagination in second language education, consider alternative structures that facilitate social relations in the classroom, and give high value to children's home languages and cultures. I hope that this work will lead to classrooms and schools where all children, but especially Hari and other English language learners, can both learn effectively and concurrently negotiate identities of power and possibility in a climate of respect, care and trust for one another.

Notes

1. I should note herein that researchers in bilingual/multilingual education use psychoanalytic constructs of identification and resistance to hypothesize why minority language children do or do not fare well in school (Cummins, 1996, 2000; Nieto, 1999). In the field of psychoanalysis, Amati-Mehler *et al.* (1993) examine the psychology of the multilingual person, drawing on a long line of work in this area and closing with a discussion of the relevance to their work of Bakhtin's theories on the dialogicality of language and the self.

References

Amati-Mehler, J., Argentieri, S. and Canestri, J. (1993) *The Babel of the Unconscious. Mother Tongue and Foreign Languages in the Psychoanalytic Dimension* (J. Whitelaw-Cucco, trans.). Madison, CT: International Universities Press.

Angélil-Carter, S. (1997) Second language acquisition of spoken and written English: Acquiring the skeptron. *TESOL Quarterly* 31, 263–287.

Antón, M. (1999) The discourse of a learner-centered classroom: Sociocultural perspectives on teacher–learner interaction in the second language classroom. *The Modern Language Journal* 83, 303–318.

Antón, M. and DiCamilla, F. (1998) Socio-cognitive functions of L1 collaborative interaction in the L2 classroom. *The Canadian Modern Language Review* 54, 314–342.

Bakhtin, M.M. (1981) *The Dialogic Imagination: Four Essays* (C. Emerson and M. Holquist, trans.). Austin, TX: University of Texas Press.

Bakhtin, M.M. (1984a) *Esthétique de la création verbale.* Paris: Gallimard.

Bakhtin, M.M. (1984b) *Problems of Dostoevsky's Poetics* (C. Emerson, trans.). Minneapolis, MN: University of Minnesota Press.

Bakhtin, M.M. (1986) *Speech Genres and Other Late Essays* (V. McGee, trans.). Austin, TX: University of Texas Press.

Bell, J. (1995) The relationship between L1 and L2 literacy: Some complicating factors. *TESOL Quarterly* 29, 687–704.

Bell, J. (1997a) *Literacy, Culture and Identity.* New York: Peter Lang.

Bell, J. (1997b) Teacher research in second and foreign language education. *The Canadian Modern Language Review* 54, 3–10.

Blackledge, A. (2000) *Literacy, Power and Social Justice.* Stoke on Trent, England: Trentham Books.

Bordo, S. (1990) Feminism, postmodernism, and gender skepticism. In L. Nicholson (ed.) *Feminism/Postmodernism* (pp. 133–156). New York: Routledge.

Bourdieu, P. (1977) The economics of linguistic exchanges. *Social Science Information* 16, 645–668.

Bourdieu, P. (1979) *Distinction: A Social Critique of the Judgment of Taste* (R. Nice, trans.). London: Routledge and Kegan Paul.

Bourdieu, P. (1991) *Language and Symbolic Power.* Cambridge, MA: Harvard University Press.

Bourne, J. (1988) 'Natural acquisition' and a 'Masked pedagogy.' *Applied Linguistics* 9, 83–99.

Bourne, J. (1992) Inside a multilingual primary classroom: A teacher, children and theories at work. PhD thesis, University of Southampton.

Bruner, J. (1990) *Acts of Meaning.* Cambridge, MA: Harvard University Press.

Canagarajah, A.S. (1993) Critical ethnography of a Sri Lankan classroom:

Ambiguities in student opposition to reproduction through ESOL. *TESOL Quarterly* 27, 601–626.

Carrington, V. and Luke, A. (1997) Literacy and Bourdieu's sociological theory: A reframing. *Language and Education* 11, 96–112.

Cazden, C. (1989) Contributions of the Bakhtin Circle to 'Communicative competence.' *Applied Linguistics* 10, 116–127.

Cazden, C. (1992) *Whole Language Plus*. New York: Teachers College Press.

Chomsky, N. (1957) *Syntactic Structures*. The Hague: Mouton.

Chomsky, N. (1965) *Aspects of the Theory of Syntax*. Cambridge, MA: MIT Press.

Cole, M. (1995) The supra-individual envelope of development: Activity and practice, situation and context. In J. Goodnow, P. Miller and F. Kessel (eds) *Cultural Practices as Contexts for Development* (pp. 105–118). San Francisco: Jossey-Bass.

Cole, M. (1996) *Cultural Psychology*. Cambridge, MA: The Belknap Press of Harvard University Press.

Cole, M., Engeström, Y. and Vasquez, O. (1997) *Mind, Culture, and Activity*. New York: Cambridge University Press.

Corder, S.P. (1967) The significance of learners' errors. *International Review of Applied Linguistics* 5, 161–70.

Corson, D. (1993) *Language, Minority Education and Gender*. Clevedon: Multilingual Matters.

Coulter, D. (1999) The epic and the novel: Dialogism and teacher research. *Educational Researcher* 28, 4–13.

Cumming, A. (1994) Alternatives in TESOL Research: Descriptive, interpretive, and ideological orientations. *TESOL Quarterly* 28, 673–703.

Cummins, J. (1996) *Negotiating Identities: Education for Empowerment in a Diverse Society*. Ontario, CA: California Association for Bilingual Education.

Cummins, J. (2000) *Language, Power and Pedagogy: Bilingual Children in the Crossfire*. Clevedon: Multilingual Matters.

Dabène, L. (1994) *Repères sociolinguistiques pour l'enseignement des langues*. Paris: Hachette.

Dabène, L. and Moore, D. (1995) Bilingual speech of migrant people. In L. Milroy and P. Muysken (eds) *One Speaker, Two Languages* (pp. 17–44). New York: Cambridge University Press.

Dagenais, D. and Day, E. (1998) Classroom language experiences of trilingual children in French Immersion. *The Canadian Modern Language Review* 54, 376–93.

Dagenais, D. and Day, E. (1999) Home language practices of trilingual children in French Immersion. *The Canadian Modern Language Review* 56, 99–123.

Davies, B. (1982) *Life in the Classroom and Playground*. Boston: Routledge and Kegan Paul.

Davies, B. (1989) *Frogs and Snails and Feminist Tales*. Boston: Allen and Unwin.

Davies, B. (1993) *Shards of Glass: Children Reading and Writing beyond Gendered Identities*. Cresskill, NJ: Hampton Press.

Davis, K. (1992) Validity and reliability in qualitative research on second language acquisition and teaching. Another researcher comments … *TESOL Quarterly* 26, 605–8.

Davis, K. (1995) Qualitative theory and methods in applied linguistics research. *TESOL Quarterly* 29, 427–453.

Day, E. (1998) Ethnographic study of kindergarten ESL learners: The roles of repetition and language play. Paper presented at the American Association of Applied Linguistics Annual Conference, Seattle, WA, March 1998.

Day, E. (1999) Identity formation in a kindergarten English language learner: An ethnographic study. PhD thesis, Simon Fraser University.

Day, E. and Shapson, S. (1996) *Studies in Immersion Education*. Clevedon: Multilingual Matters.

Denos, C. (in press) Jennifer: Negotiating powerful positions in a primary classroom. *Language Arts*.

Denos, C., Hof, L., Ilieva, R., Rowbotham, S., Sandhu, S., Thompson, J., Toohey, K., Tsoukalas, C. and Waterstone, B. (2001) Shifting centres of expertise: Diversity in classroom and research communities. Paper presented at the Annual Meeting of the American Educational Research Association, April 2001, Seattle, WA.

Denos, C., Hof, L., Ilieva, R., Rowbotham, S., Sandhu, S., Tsoukalas, C. and Waterstone, B. (in press) A Teacher Action Research Group's response to 'Breaking them up, taking them away': ESL students in Grade 1. In J. Sharkey, C. Lazer and K. Johnson (eds) *Teacher–research Dialogues: Rethinking Issues of Language, Culture and Power*.

Deprez, C. (1994) *Les enfants bilingues: langues et familles*. Paris: Didier.

Dewey, J. (1989) *Experience and Nature*. La Salle, IL: Open Court Press.

Donato, R. (1994) Collective scaffolding in second language learning. In J. Lantolf and G. Appel (eds) *Vygotskian Approaches to Second Language Research* (pp. 33–56). Norwood, NJ: Ablex.

Donato, R. and McCormick, D. (1994) A sociocultural perspective on language learning strategies: The role of mediation. *The Modern Language Journal* 78, 453–464.

Duff, P. (1995) An ethnography of communication in immersion classrooms in Hungary. *TESOL Quarterly* 29, 505–537.

Dulay, H., Burt, M. and Krashen, S. (1982) *Language Two*. New York: Oxford University Press.

Dunn, W. and Lantolf, J. (1998) Vygotsky's Zone of proximal development and Krashen's *i* + 1: Incommensurable constructs; incommensurable theories. *Language Learning* 48, 411–442.

Duranti, A. and Goodwin, C. (eds) (1992) *Rethinking Context: Language as an Interactive Phenomenon*. New York: Cambridge University Press.

Dyson, A. (1997) *Writing Superheroes. Contemporary Childhood, Popular Culture, and Classroom Literacy*. New York: Teachers College Press.

Dyson, A. and Genishi, C. (1994) *The Need for Story*. Urbana, IL: National Council of Teachers of English.

Eisenhart, M. (1995) The fax, the jazz player, and the self-story teller: How *do* people organize culture? *Anthropology and Education Quarterly* 26, 3–26.

Ellis, R. (1985) *Understanding Second Language Acquisition*. New York: Oxford University Press.

Ellis, R. (1990) *Instructed Second Language Acquisition*. Cambridge, MA: Basil Blackwell.

Ellis, R. (1994) *The Study of Second Language Acquisition*. New York: Oxford University Press.

Faltis, C. and Hudelson, S. (1998) *Bilingual Education in Elementary and Secondary School Communities. Toward Understanding and Caring*. Boston: Allyn and Bacon.

Firth, A. and Wagner, J. (1997) On discourse, communication, and (some) fundamental concepts in SLA research. *The Modern Language Journal* 81, 285–300.

Forman, E., Minick, N. and Stone, C.A. (eds) (1993) *Contexts for Learning*. New York: Oxford University Press.

Freire, P. (1985) *The Politics of Education: Culture, Power, and Liberation*. South Hadley, MA: Bergin and Garvey.

Gardner, R. (1985) *Social Psychology and Second Language Learning: The Role of Attitudes and Motivation*. London: Edward Arnold.

Gass, S. and Madden, C. (1985) *Input in Second Language Acquisition*. Rowley, MA: Newbury House.

Geertz, C. (1973) *The Interpretation of Cultures*. New York: Basic Books.

Geertz, C. (1976) 'From the native's point of view': On the nature of anthropological understanding. In K.H. Basso and H.A. Selby (eds) *Meaning in Anthropology* (pp. 221–237). Albuquerque, NM: University of New Mexico Press.

Goetz, J. and LeCompte, M. (1984) *Ethnography and Qualitative Design in Educational Research*. Orlando, FL: Academic Press.

Goodnow, J. (1990a) The socialization of cognition: What's involved? In J. Stigler, R. Shweder and G. Herdt (eds) *Cultural Psychology. Essays on Comparative Human Development* (pp. 259–286). New York: Cambridge University Press.

Goodnow, J. (1990b) Using sociology to extend psychological accounts of cognitive development. *Human Development* 33, 81–107.

Goodwin, M. (1990) *He-said-she-said. Talk as Social Organization among Black Children*. Bloomington, IN: Indiana University Press.

Gould, S.J. (1987) Animals and us. *The New York Review of Books*, June 25, 20–25.

Graue, M.E. and Walsh, D.J. (1998) *Studying Children in Context*. Thousand Oaks, CA: Sage.

Gumperz, J. (1982) *Discourse Strategies*. New York: Cambridge University Press.

Gutierrez, K. (1993) Biliteracy and the language-minority child. In B. Spodek and O. Saracho (eds) *Language and Literacy in Early Childhood Education* (pp. 82–101). New York: Teachers College Press.

Gutierrez, K. (1994) How talk, context, and script shape contexts for learning: A cross-case comparison of journal sharing. *Linguistics and Education* 5, 335–365.

Gutierrez, K. and Larson, J. (1994) Language borders: Recitation as hegemonic discourse. *International Journal of Educational Reform* 3, 22–36.

Gutierrez, K., Rymes, B. and Larson, J. (1995) *Script, Counterscript, and Underlife in the Classroom: James Brown versus Brown v. Board of Education*. *Harvard Educational Review* 65, 445–471.

Hall, J.K. (1993a) The role of oral practices in the accomplishment of our everyday lives: The sociocultural dimension of interaction with implications for the learning of another language. *Applied Linguistics* 14, 145–166.

Hall, J.K. (1993b) *Oye oye lo que ustedes no saben:* Creativity, social power, and politics in the oral practice of *chismeando*. *Journal of Linguistic Anthropology* 3, 75–98.

Hall, J.K. (1995) (Re)creating our worlds with words: A sociohistorical perspective of face-to-face interaction. *Applied Linguistics* 16, 206–232.

Hall, J.K. (1997) A consideration of SLA as a theory of practice: A response to Firth and Wagner. *The Modern Language Journal* 81, 301–306.

Hall, J.K. (1998) Differential teacher attention to student utterances: The construction of different opportunities for learning in the IRF. *Linguistics and Education* 9, 287–311.

Hall, J.K. and Verplaetse, L.S. (2000) *Second and Foreign Language Learning through Classroom Interaction*. Mahwah, NJ: Lawrence Erlbaum.

Hall, S. (1990) Cultural identity and diaspora. In J. Rutherford (ed.) *Identity: Community, Culture, Difference* (pp. 222–237). London: Lawrence and Wishart.

Hall, S. (1996) Introduction: Who needs identity? In S. Hall and P. du Gay (eds) *Questions of Cultural Identity* (pp. 1–17). London: Sage.

Hammersley, M. and Atkinson, P. (1983) *Ethnography. Principles in Practice*. New York: Tavistock.

Haneda, M. (1997) Second language learning in a 'community of practice': A case study of adult Japanese learners. *The Canadian Modern Language Review* 54, 11–27.

Hanks, W. (1996) *Language and Communicative Practices*. Boulder, CO: Westview Press.

Heller, M. (1987) The role of language in the formation of ethnic identity. In J. Phinney and M. Rotheram (eds) *Children's Ethnic Socialization* (pp. 180–200). Newbury Park: Sage.

Heller, M. (1995) Language choice, social institutions, and symbolic domination. *Language in Society* 24, 373–405.

Henriques, J., Hollway, W., Urwin, C., Venn, C. and Walkerdine, V. (1984) *Changing the Subject*. New York: Methuen.

Hodges, D. (1998) Participation as dis-identification with/in a community of practice. *Mind, Culture, and Activity* 5, 272–290.

Holland, D., Lachicotte, W., Skinner, D. and Cain, C. (1998) *Identity and Agency in Cultural Worlds*. Cambridge, MA: Harvard University Press.

Holquist, M. (1990) *Dialogism. Bakhtin and His World*. New York: Routledge.

Hunter, J. (1997) Multiple perceptions: Social identity in a multilingual elementary classroom. *TESOL Quarterly* 31, 603–611.

Hymes, D. (1974) Ways of speaking. In R. Bauman and J. Sherzer (eds) *Explorations in the Ethnography of Speaking* (pp. 433–451). London: Cambridge University Press.

Ibrahim, A. (1999) Becoming black: Rap and hip-hop, race, gender, identity and the politics of ESL learning. *TESOL Quarterly* 33, 349–369.

James, A., Jenks, C. and Prout, A. (1998) *Theorizing Childhood*. Cambridge, England: Polity Press.

John-Steiner, V. and Mahn, H. (1996) Sociocultural approaches to learning and development: A Vygotskian framework. *Educational Psychologist* 31, 191–206.

Kanno, Y. (2000) Kikokushijo as bicultural. *International Journal of Intercultural Relations* 24, 361–382.

Kanno, Y. and Applebaum, S. (1995) ESL students speak up: Their stories of how we are doing. *TESL Canada Journal* 12, 32–49.

Kirshner, D. and Whitson, J. (1997) Editors' introduction to Situated Cognition. In D. Kirshner and J. Whitson (eds) *Situated Cognition. Social, Semiotic, and Psychological Perspectives* (pp. 1–16). Mahwah, NJ: Lawrence Erlbaum.

Krashen, S. (1981) *Second Language Acquisition and Second Language Learning*. New York: Oxford University Press.

Kress, G. (1989) *Linguistic Processes in Sociocultural Practice*. Oxford: Oxford University Press.

Lacan, J. (1977) *Ecrits: A Selection*. New York: W.W. Norton.

Lantolf, J. (1996) SLA theory building: 'Letting all the flowers bloom!' *Language Learning* 46, 713–749.

Lantolf, J. (2000) *Sociocultural Theory and Second Language Learning.* New York: Oxford University Press.

Lantolf, J. and Appel, G. (eds) (1994a) *Vygotskian Approaches to Second Language Research.* Norwood, NJ: Ablex.

Lantolf, J. and Appel, G. (1994b) Theoretical framework: An introduction to Vygotskian approaches to second language research. In J. Lantolf and G. Appel (eds) *Vygotskian Approaches to Second Language Research* (pp. 1–32). Norwood, NJ: Ablex.

Lantolf, J. and Pavlenko, A. (1995) Sociocultural theory and second language acquisition. *Annual Review of Applied Linguistics* 15, 108–124.

Larsen-Freeman, D. and Long, M. (1991) *An Introduction to Second Language Acquisition Research.* New York: Longman.

Lave, J. (1996) Teaching, as learning, in practice. *Mind, Culture, and Activity* 3, 149–164.

Lave, J. and Wenger, E. (1991) *Situated Learning. Legitimate Peripheral Participation.* New York: Cambridge University Press.

Lazaraton, A. (1995) Qualitative research in applied linguistics: A progress report. *TESOL Quarterly* 29, 455–471.

Lemke, J. (1995) *Textual Politics: Discourse and Social Dynamics.* London: Taylor & Francis.

LePage, R.B. and Tabouret-Keller, A. (1985) *Acts of Identity: Creole-based Approaches to Language and Ethnicity.* New York: Cambridge University Press.

Leung, C., Harris, R. and Rampton, B. (1997) The idealised native speaker, reified ethnicities, and classroom realities. *TESOL Quarterly* 31, 543–560.

Lin, A.M.Y. (1996) Doing-English-lessons in secondary schools in Hong Kong: A sociocultural and discourse-analytic approach. PhD thesis, University of Toronto.

Lin, A.M.Y. (1999) Doing-English-lessons in the reproduction or transformation of social worlds? *TESOL Quarterly* 33, 393–412.

Lincoln, Y. and Guba, E. (1985) *Naturalistic Inquiry.* Beverly Hills, CA: Sage.

Litowitz, B. (1993) Deconstruction in the zone of proximal development. In E. Forman, N. Minick and C.A. Stone (eds) *Contexts for Learning* (pp. 184–196). New York: Oxford University Press.

Litowitz, B. (1997) Just say no: Responsibility and resistance. In M. Cole, Y. Engeström and O. Vasquez (eds) *Mind, Culture, and Activity* (pp. 473–484). New York: Cambridge University Press.

Maclean, R. (1996) Quick! Hide! Constructing a playground identity in the early weeks of school. *Language and Education* 10, 171–186.

McCarty, T. (1997) Teacher research methods in language and education. In N. Hornberger and D. Corson (eds) *Encyclopedia of Language and Education,* Vol. 8 (pp. 227–237). Dordrecht: Kluwer Academic Publishers.

McDermott, R. (1993) The acquisition of a child by a learning disability. In S. Chaiklin and J. Lave (eds) *Understanding Practice* (pp. 269–305). New York: Cambridge University Press.

McGroarty, M. (1998) Constructive and constructivist challenges for applied linguistics. *Language Learning* 48, 591–622.

McKay, S. and Wong, S. (1996) Multiple discourses, multiple identities: Investment and agency in second-language learning among Chinese adolescent immigrant students. *Harvard Educational Review* 66, 577–608.

Marková, I. and Foppa, K. (1990) *The Dynamics of Dialogue*. New York: Harvester Wheatsheaf.

Matusov, E. (1996) Intersubjectivity without agreement. *Mind, Culture, and Activity* 3, 25–45.

Merriam, S. (1988) *Case Study Research in Education*. San Francisco: Jossey-Bass.

Miller, J. (1999) Becoming audible: Social identity and second language use. *Journal of Intercultural Studies* 20, 149–165.

Miller, J. (2000) Language use, identity, and social interaction: Migrant students in Australia. *Research on Language and Social Interaction* 33, 69–100.

Miller, P. and Goodnow, J. (1995) Cultural practices: Toward an integration of culture and development. In J. Goodnow, P. Miller and F. Kessel (eds) *Cultural Practices as Contexts for Development* (pp. 5–16). San Francisco: Jossey-Bass.

Milroy, L. and Muysken, P. (1995) *One Speaker, Two Languages*. New York: Cambridge University Press.

Minick, N., Stone, C.A. and Forman, E. (1993) Introduction: Integration of individual, social, and institutional processes in accounts of children's learning and development. In E. Forman, N. Minick and C.A. Stone (eds) *Contexts for Learning* (pp. 3–16). New York: Oxford University Press.

Mitchell, R. and Myles, F. (1998) *Second Language Learning Theories*. New York: Oxford University Press.

Morgan, B. (1987) Three dreams of language; Or, No longer immured in the Bastille of the humanist word. *College English* 49, 449–458.

Nieto, S. (1999) *The Light in their Eyes. Creating Multicultural Learning Communities*. New York: Teachers College Press.

Norton Peirce, B. (1989) Toward a pedagogy of possibility in the teaching of English internationally: People's English in South Africa. *TESOL Quarterly* 23, 401–420.

Norton Peirce, B. (1993) Language learning, social identity, and immigrant women. PhD thesis, University of Toronto.

Norton Peirce, B. (1995) Social identity, investment, and language learning. *TESOL Quarterly* 29, 9–31.

Norton, B. (ed.) (1997a) Language and identity. *TESOL Quarterly Special Issue* 31 (3).

Norton, B. (1997b) Language, identity, and the ownership of English. *TESOL Quarterly* 31, 409–429.

Norton, B. (2000) *Identity and Language Learning: Gender, Ethnicity and Educational Change*. London: Longman.

Norton, B. (2001) Non-participation, imagined communities and the language classroom. In M. Breen (ed.) *Learner Contributions to Language Learning. New Directions in Research* (pp. 159–171). New York: Longman.

Norton, B. and Toohey, K. (2001) Changing conceptions of good language learners: A window on SLA theory. *TESOL Quarterly* 35, 307–322.

Ochs, E. (1988) *Culture and Language Development*. New York: Cambridge University Press.

Ochs, E. (ed.) (1991) Socialization through language and interaction (Special issue). *Issues in Applied Linguistics* 2 (1).

Ochs, E. (1993) Constructing social identity: A language socialization perspective. *Research on Language and Social Interaction* 26, 287–306.

Ochs, E. (1996) Linguistic resources for socializing humanity. In J. Gumperz and S. Levinson (eds) *Rethinking Linguistic Relativity* (pp. 407–437). New York: Cambridge University Press.

Orellana, M. (1994) Appropriating the voice of the superheroes: Three preschoolers' bilingual language uses in play. *Early Childhood Research Quarterly* 9, 171–193.

Ortiz, F. (1988) Hispanic-American children's experiences in classrooms: A comparison between Hispanic and non-Hispanic children. In L. Weis (ed.) *Class, Race, and Gender in American Education* (pp. 63–86). Albany, NY: State University of New York Press.

Packer, M. (1993) Away from internalization. In E. Forman, N. Minick and C.A. Stone (eds) *Contexts for Learning* (pp. 254–265). New York: Oxford University Press.

Paley, V.G. (1992) *You Can't Say You Can't Play*. Cambridge, MA: Harvard University Press.

Pappas, C. (1999) Becoming literate in the borderlands. In A. Göncü (ed.) *Children's Engagement in the World* (pp. 228–260). New York: Cambridge University Press.

Pappas, C. and Zecker, L. (2001) *Teacher Inquiries in Literacy Teaching-Learning. Learning to Collaborate in Elementary Urban Classrooms*. Mahwah, NJ: Lawrence Erlbaum.

Pavlenko, A. (2000) Access to linguistic resources: Key variable in second language learning. *Estudios de Sociolingüística* 1, 85–105.

Pavlenko, A. and Lantolf, J. (2000) Second language learning as participation and the (re) construction of selves. In J. Lantolf (ed.) *Sociocultural Theory and Second Language Learning* (pp. 155–177). New York: Oxford University Press.

Pease-Alvarez, L. and Winsler, A. (1994) Cuando el maestro no habla español: Children's bilingual language practices in the classroom. *TESOL Quarterly* 28, 507–535.

Pennycook, A. (1990) Toward a critical applied linguistics for the 1990s. *Issues in Applied Linguistics* 1, 8–28.

Pennycook, A. (2001) *Critical Applied Linguistics*. Mahwah, NJ: Lawrence Erlbaum.

Pica, T. (1994) Research on negotiation: What does it reveal about second-language learning conditions, processes, and outcomes? *Language Learning* 44, 493–527.

Platt, E. and Brooks, F. (1994) The 'Acquisition-rich environment' revisited. *The Modern Language Journal* 78, 497–511.

Platt, E. and Troudi, S. (1997) Mary and her teachers: A Grebo-speaking child's place in the mainstream classroom. *The Modern Language Journal* 81, 28–49.

Poole, D. (1992) Language socialization in the second language classroom. *Language Learning* 42, 593–616.

Price, S. (1996) Comments on Bonny Norton Peirce's 'Social identity, investment, and language learning.' A reader reacts … *TESOL Quarterly* 30, 331–337.

Ramanathan, V. and Atkinson, D. (1999) Ethnographic approaches and methods in L2 writing research: A critical guide and review. *Applied Linguistics* 20, 44–70.

Rampton, B. (1991) Second language learners in a stratified multilingual setting. *Applied Linguistics* 12, 229–248.

Rampton, B. (1995) *Crossing: Language and Ethnicity Among Adolescents*. London: Longman.

Reddy, M. (1979) The conduit metaphor. In A. Ortony (ed.) *Metaphor and Thought* (pp. 284–324). Cambridge: Cambridge University Press.

Richardson, V. (1994) Conducting research on practice. *Educational Researcher* 23, 5–10.

Rizzo, T.A. (1989) *Friendship Development among Children in School.* Norwood, NJ: Ablex.

Rodby, J. (1992) *Appropriating Literacy: Writing and Reading in English as a Second Language.* Portsmouth, NH: Boynton/Cook.

Rogoff, B. (1990) *Apprenticeship in Thinking.* New York: Oxford University Press.

Rogoff, B. (1994) Developing understanding of the idea of communities of learners. *Mind, Culture, and Activity* 1, 209–229.

Rogoff, B., Mosier, C., Mistry, J. and Göncü, A. (1993) Toddlers' guided participation with their caregivers in cultural activity. In E. Forman, N. Minick and C.A. Stone (eds) *Contexts for Learning* (pp. 230–253). New York: Oxford University Press.

Rymes, B. (1997) Second language socialization: A new approach to second language acquisition research. *Journal of Intensive English Studies* 11, 143–155.

Saravia-Shore, M. and Arvizu, S. (1992) *Cross-cultural Literacy.* New York: Garland Publishing.

Schecter, S. and Bayley, R. (1997) Language socialization practices and cultural identity: Case studies of Mexican-descent families in California and Texas. *TESOL Quarterly* 31, 513–541.

Schieffelin, B. and Ochs, E. (1986) Language socialization. *Annual Review of Anthropology* 15, 163–191.

Schumann, J. (1978a) *The Pidginisation Process: A Model for Second Language Acquisition.* Rowley, MA: Newbury House.

Schumann, J. (1978b) The acculturation model for second-language acquisition. In R. Gingras (ed.) *Second Language Acquisition and Foreign Language Teaching* (pp. 27–50). Washington, DC: Center for Applied Linguistics.

Selinker, L. (1972) Interlanguage. *International Review of Applied Linguistics* 10, 209–31.

Shweder, R. (1984) Preview: A colloquy of culture theorists. In R. Shweder and R. LeVine (eds) *Culture Theory: Essays on Mind, Self, and Emotion* (pp. 1–24). New York: Cambridge University Press.

Siegal, M. (1996) The role of learner subjectivity in second language sociolinguistic competency: Western women learning Japanese. *Applied Linguistics* 17, 356–382.

Skeggs, B. (1995) Theorizing, ethics and representation in feminist ethnography. In B. Skeggs (ed.) *Feminist Cultural Theory* (pp. 190–206). New York: Manchester University Press.

Smolka, A., De Goes, M. and Pino, A. (1995) The constitution of the subject. In J. Wertsch, P. del Río and A. Alvarez. (eds) *Sociocultural Studies of Mind* (pp. 165–184). New York: Cambridge University Press.

Stone, C.A. (1993) What is missing in the metaphor of scaffolding? In E. Forman, N. Minick and C.A. Stone (eds) *Contexts for Learning* (pp. 169–183). New York: Oxford University Press.

Swain, M. (1985) Communicative competence: Some roles of comprehensible input and comprehensible output in its development. In S. Gass and C. Madden (eds) *Input in Second Language Acquisition* (pp. 235–253). Rowley, MA: Newbury House.

Swain, M. (2000) The output hypothesis and beyond: Mediating acquisition through collaborative dialogue. In J. Lantolf (ed.) *Sociocultural Theory and Second Language Learning* (pp. 97–114). New York: Oxford University Press.

Swain, M. and Lapkin, S. (1998) Interaction in second language learning: Two adolescent French immersion students working together. *Modern Language Journal* 82, 320–337.

Tannen, D. (1989) *Talking Voices*. New York: Cambridge University Press.

Taylor, C. (1985) *Human Agency and Language*. New York: Cambridge University Press.

Taylor, C. (1989) *Sources of the Self*. Cambridge, MA: Harvard University Press.

Taylor, C. (1993) To follow a rule. In C. Calhoun, E. LiPuma and M. Postone (eds) *Bourdieu: Critical Perspectives* (pp. 45–60). Chicago: The University of Chicago Press.

Thesen, L. (1997) Voices, discourse and transition: In search of new categories in EAP. *TESOL Quarterly* 31, 487–511.

Toohey, K. (1996) Learning English as a second language in kindergarten: A community of practice perspective. *The Canadian Modern Language Review* 52, 549–576.

Toohey, K. (1998) 'Breaking them up, taking them away': ESL students in grade one. *TESOL Quarterly* 32, 61–84.

Toohey, K. (2000) *Learning English at School: Identity, Social Relations and Classroom Practice*. Clevedon: Multilingual Matters.

Toohey, K. and Day, E. (1999) Language-learning: The importance of access to community. *TESL Canada Journal* 17, 40–53.

Toohey, K. and Waterstone, B. (2001, April) 'Telling ... or ... asking for help': Negotiations of position in an action research community. Paper presented at the Annual Meeting of the American Educational Research Association, Seattle, WA.

Toohey, K., Waterstone, B. and Julé-Lemke, A. (2000) Community of learners, carnival and participation in a Punjabi Sikh classroom. *The Canadian Modern Language Review* 56, 421–436.

Trueba, H., Guthrie, G.P. and Au, K. (eds) (1981) *Culture and the Bilingual Classroom: Studies in Classroom Ethnography*. Rowley, MA: Newbury House.

Urwin, C. (1984) Power relations and the emergence of language. In J. Henriques, W. Hollway, C. Urwin, C. Venn and V. Walkerdine (eds) *Changing the Subject* (pp. 264–322). New York: Methuen.

van Lier, L. (2000) From input to affordance: Social-interactive learning from an ecological perspective. In J. Lantolf (ed.) *Sociocultural Theory and Second Language Learning* (pp. 245–259). New York: Oxford University Press.

Van Maanen, J. (1995) *Representation in Ethnography*. Thousand Oaks, CA: Sage.

Vasquez, O., Pease-Alvarez, L. and Shannon, S. (1994) *Pushing Boundaries: Language and Culture in a Mexicano Community*. New York: Cambridge University Press.

Vygotsky, L.S. (1978) *Mind in Society*. Cambridge, MA: Harvard University Press.

Vygotsky. L.S. (1981) The genesis of higher mental functions. In J. Wertsch (ed.) *The Concept of Activity in Soviet Psychology*. Armonck, New York: M.E. Sharpe.

Vygotsky, L.S. (1986) *Thought and Language* (A. Kozulin, trans.). Cambridge, MA: MIT Press.

Walkerdine, V. (1997) Redefining the subject in situated cognition theory. In D. Kirshner and J. Whitson (eds) *Situated Cognition. Social, Semiotic, and Psychological Perspectives* (pp. 57–70). Mahwah, NJ: Lawrence Erlbaum.

Waterstone, B. (2001, February) More than just 'inclusion': The 'interanimation' of difference in Bakhtin's dialogic. Paper presented at National Council of Teachers of English Midwinter Assembly, Berkeley, CA.

Watson-Gegeo, K.A. (1988) Ethnography in ESL: Defining the essentials. *TESOL Quarterly* 22, 575–592.

Weedon, C. (1987) *Feminist Practice and Poststructuralist Theory.* New York: Basil Blackwell.

Wells, G. (1994) *Changing Schools from Within. Creating Communities of Inquiry.* Toronto: Oise Press.

Wells, G. (1999) *Dialogic Inquiry: Towards a Sociocultural Practice and Theory of Education.* New York: Cambridge University Press.

Wells, G. and Chang-Wells, G.L. (1992) *Constructing Knowledge Together.* Portsmouth, NH: Heineman.

Wenger, E. (1998) *Communities of Practice: Learning, Meaning, and Identity.* New York: Cambridge University Press.

Wertsch, J.V. (1991) *Voices of the Mind.* Cambridge, MA: Harvard University Press.

White, L. (1989) *Universal Grammar and Second Language Acquisition.* Amsterdam: John Benjamins.

Willett, J. (1995) Becoming first graders in an L2: An ethnographic study of L2 socialization. *TESOL Quarterly* 29, 473–503.

Willett, J., Solsken, J. and Wilson-Keenan, J. (1999) The (im)possibilities of constructing multicultural language practices in research and pedagogy. *Linguistics and Education* 10, 165–218.

Winnicott, D. (1971) *Playing and Reality.* New York: Basic Books.

Wong Fillmore, L. (1979) Individual differences in second language acquisition. In C. Fillmore, D. Kempler and W. Wang (eds) *Individual Differences in Language Ability and Language Behavior* (pp. 203–228). New York: Academic Press.

Wong Fillmore, L. (1989) Language learning in social context. The view from research in second language learning. In R. Dietrich and C.F. Graumann (eds) *Language Processing in Social Context* (pp. 277–302). Amsterdam: North-Holland.

Wood, D., Bruner, J.S. and Ross, G. (1976) The role of tutoring in problem-solving. *Journal of Child Psychology and Psychiatry* 17, 89–100.

Appendix: Transcription Conventions[1]

Square brackets indicate the onset of simultaneous and/or overlapping utterances:

Example:

Child: [Stone, rone.
Some children: [Stone, bone.

Equals signs indicate contiguous utterances, in which the second is latched onto the first; or an utterance that continues beyond an overlapping utterance.

Example:

Hari: There got lots of colors=
Casey: =Yea

One or more colons (::) represent an extension of the sound syllable it follows (see following example).

Underlining indicates emphasis.

Example:

No::: you can't put it here

Capital letters indicate loudness.

Example:

RED, purple, RED, purple, RED

Pauses and details of the conversational scenes or various characterizations of the talk are inserted in single parentheses and italicized.

Example:

Teacher: *(acknowledging Hari)* Right, I heard it.

Items enclosed within single parentheses and **not** italicized indicate transcriptionist doubt.

Example:

Casey: The dirt bike, yea: (you're going) on the motorcycle.

Other than the above conventions, I have used the standard English alphabet to represent casual speech in the way that it is represented in literary works where the author wishes the reader to hear a particular pronunciation.

Example:

Hari: I wanna go.

Note

1. These conventions have been adapted from Ochs (1996: 432–433).

Index

Authors

Shapson, S., 3
Shweder, R., 35
Siegal, M., 22, 52, 71
Skeggs, B., 1, 32, 33
Smolka, A., 10, 16, 69
Stone, C.A., 14, 105, 107n
Swain, M., 9-10, 14

Tabouret-Keller, A., 52
Tannen, D., 28
Taylor, C., 4, 16
Thesen, L., 107
Toohey, K., 4-5, 7n, 9-10, 22, 24-25, 28, 31, 36, 71, 86-87, 89n, 106, 111-112, 115
Troudi, S., 22
Trueba, H., 21

Urwin, C., 27n, 71, 106

van Lier, L., 10
Van Maanen, J., 115
Vasquez, O., 22, 52, 111, 114
Verplaetse, L.S., 10, 113

Vygotsky, L.S., 6, 10, 12-14, 16-17, 20, 22, 26, 103-104, 108

Wagner, J., 10, 110-111
Walkerdine, V., 19, 95, 106, 110
Walsh, D.J., 32-33
Waterstone, B., 115
Watson-Gegeo, K.A., 21
Weedon, C., 6, 18, 26, 106, 108
Wells, G., 14, 115
Wenger, E., 6, 14-17, 25-26, 55, 69, 71, 104, 108-109, 112
Wertsch, J., 12, 14, 16, 26
White, L., 9
Whitson, J., 20
Willett, J., 10, 22-23, 25, 34n, 112
Winnicott, D., 104-105
Winsler, A., 52-53
Wong, S., 22, 24, 106, 113
Wong Fillmore, L., 9, 52
Wood, D., 14

Zecker, L., 115

Subjects

Access, 5, 15, 18, 22-26, 52, 69, 72-73, 78, 87, 97, 108-109, 116
Affect, affectivity, 7, 14, 19-20, 42, 78, 90, 97, 103-104, 106-107, 109, 111, 113, 116
Appropriation, 10, 73, 82, 87-88

Community of practice, 15-17, 69, 71, 109
Context, 9, 10, 12, 19, 20-22, 26, 110-111

Degradation, 67-70
Desire, 18, 19-20, 27n, 90, 104, 106, 107, 110
Dialogue, dialogic, dialogicality, 10-11, 13, 16, 87-88, 116n
Discourse (authoritative, internally persuasive), 87

English as a second language (ESL), 1, 5, 7n, 22, 25, 38
English language learner(s), 2, 4, 5, 7n, 22, 26, 34n, 37-38, 43

– Hari, 60, 105, 108, 116
– other children, 60, 62, 65, 71, 84, 88, 94
Ethnography, ethnographic, 4, 6, 20-21, 22-24, 26, 30, 110-111, 115

Friendship, affiliation, 78, 86-87, 89, 108, 113
– *see also* Hari

Gender, 23, 34n, 66, 71

Hari
– English language use, 6, 44-54, 110
– friendship, affiliation, 52, 54-55, 60, 73, 78, 85-86, 88-89
– home language, 6, 35-36, 43-49, 52-54
– identity, 6, 45-46, 52-55, 62-65, 71-73, 76, 78, 81-82, 86-87, 108-109, 110, 112, 116
– narrative, story, 51-52, 54n, 71, 92, 97, 109